Sunderland

The Biggest Shipbuilding ~~Town in the~~ World

by

Alan Brett and Andrew Clark

An atmospheric photograph by Ken Price of the heyday of shipbuilding in Sunderland. Ken, a professional photographer, supplied a number of superb pictures for this publication.

Copyright Alan Brett & Andrew Clark 2005

First published in 2005

Black Cat Publications
163 Brandling Street
Roker
Sunderland
SR6 0LN

ISBN 1 899560 78 5

No part of this publication may be reproduced, stored in a mechanical retrieval system, or transmitted, in any form or by any means, electronic, mechanical, photocopying, recording or otherwise, without prior permission of the authors.

Contents

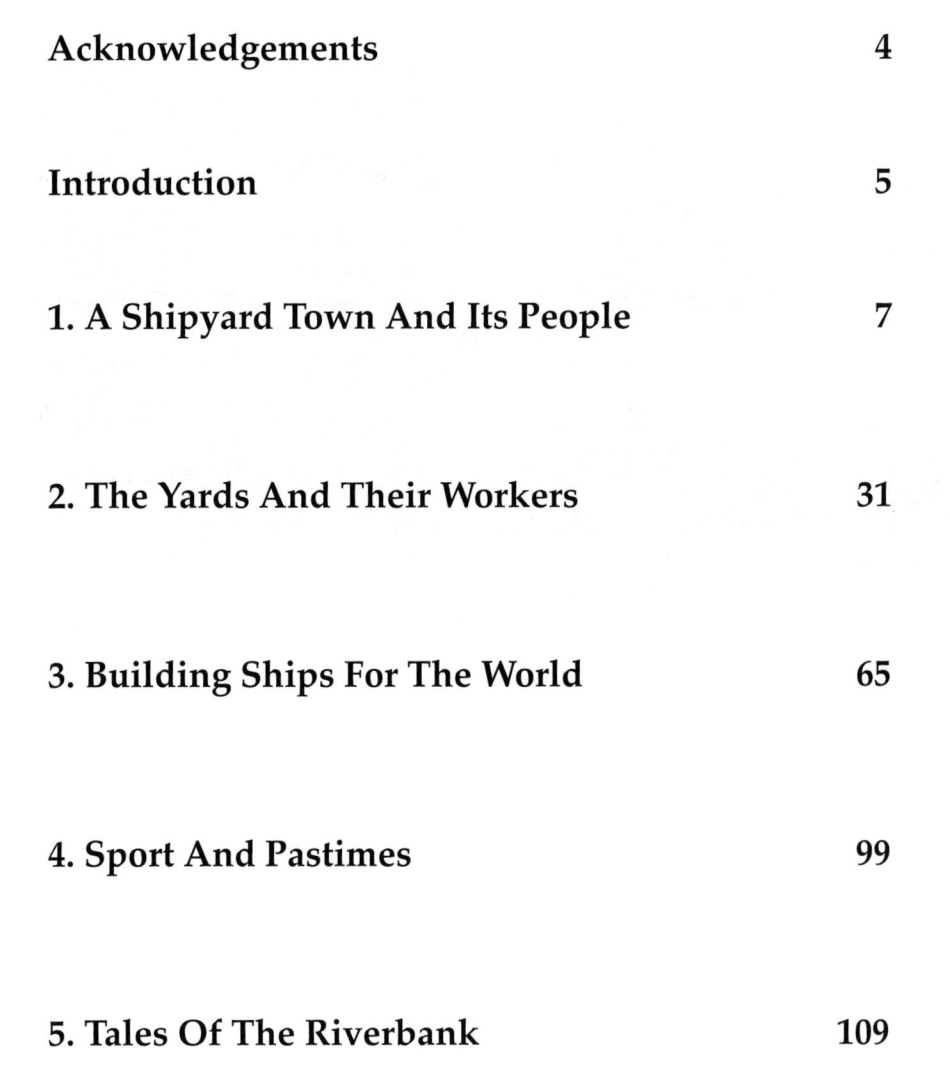

Acknowledgements 4

Introduction 5

1. A Shipyard Town And Its People 7

2. The Yards And Their Workers 31

3. Building Ships For The World 65

4. Sport And Pastimes 99

5. Tales Of The Riverbank 109

Acknowledgements

The authors would like to thank the following for their help with this publication:

Tommy Bell, Michael Bute, Ian S. Carr, Keith Cockerill, Philip Curtis, Billy Dent, Peter Gibson, Brian Holden, Edward MacKenzie, George Marrs, George Nairn, John Oliver, Alan Owen, Ken Price, Tom & Edith Richardson, John Yearnshire.

Phil Hall, Ashley Sutherland, Liz Tinker & John Wood at Sunderland City Library

Martin Routledge of Sunderland Museum

Special thanks to John Oliver for his excellent records of Sunderland ship launches.

The following photographs are by kind permission of Sunderland Museum & Winter Gardens – Tyne and Wear Museums

Cover, Page 11, Page 20 *bottom*, Page 25 *top*, Page 71 *top* and *bottom*, Page 97 *top*.

Bibliography

Kevin Brady *Sunderland's Blitz* The People's History, 1999
M. Clay, G.E. Milburn and S.T. Miller *An Eye Plan of Sunderland and Bishopwearmouth 1785-1790 by John Rain* Frank Graham, 1984
Raich Carter *Footballer's Progress* Sporting Handbooks, 1950
Keith Cockerill *Bridges of the River Wear* The People's History, 2005
C.H.G. Hopkins *Pallion 1974 to 1954: Church and People in a Shipyard Parish* C.H.G. Hopkins, 1954
John Lingwood *SD 14: The Full Story* Ships in Focus Publications, 2004
Norman L. Middlemiss *British Shipbuilding Yards Volume One North-East Coast* Shield Publications, 1993
Ray Nichols *Changing Tide – Final Years of Wear Shipbuilding* Sunderland & Hartlepool Publishing & Printing, 1990
J.W. Smith and T.S. Holden *Where Ships Are Born* Thomas Reed, 1947

Report of an Enquiry by the Board of Trade into Working Class Rents, Housing and Retail Prices, together with the Standard Rates of Wages prevailing in certain occupations in the Principal Industrial Towns of the United Kingdom. His Majesty's Stationery Office, 1906

Marwood's Maritime Directory 1851

Newspapers & Journals

A&P News
Bank Line Magazine
The London Illustrated News
The Racing Pigeon
Sunderland Echo
Sunderland Times
Sunderland Weekly News
The Syren and Shipping
The Times

Introduction

'On a narrow river with many difficult bends and corners we manage to launch more merchant ship tonnage than any other town in the world.'

W.B. Marr, chairman of Sir James Laing & Son

Sunderland once made the proud boast of being the biggest shipbuilding town in the world and this book is a celebration of that golden age. This achievement was earned through the hard work and skill of generations of Sunderland shipbuilders. The great names of Pile, Doxford, Thompson, Austin, Pickersgill, Laing, Short and Bartram are still remembered as men of 'genius' who established the industry on the banks of the Wear. They founded the shipyard firms that survived world wars, the Depression and many changes in the industry to launch some of the finest ships ever constructed. These ships were built by shipwrights, caulkers, riveters, platers and welders whose craftsmanship was the envy of the world.

At the peak of shipbuilding in Sunderland there were sometimes three launches in an hour. Those days are remembered with fondness but sadly they were not to last. The end of shipbuilding on the Wear in the 1980s saw the closure of some of the most up to date facilities in the country.

The shipyards are gone but not forgotten and this book brings to life Sunderland's great heritage.

A vessel under construction at JL Thompson's – one of the thousands of ships built in Sunderland.

The industrial skyline of Sunderland in the 1960s. This photograph was taken by former shipyard worker, Brian Holden. He is a keen amateur photographer and many of his pictures are used in this book. They capture the industry from a unique first-hand perspective.

Chapter One

A Shipyard Town And Its People

Around The River

A busy scene on the Wear from the early 1930s showing a hive of activity with tugs and ships on the river. In the background are the Wearmouth Bridge and the Railway Bridge. When men left the shipyards at the end of their working day the bridges over the Wear would be packed with workers returning home.

A postcard taken from Wearmouth Bridge in the 1950s showing two well known shipbuilding firms – Austin's and JL Thompson's. On the right is Austin's with one ship on the pontoon and one alongside. On the left is the huge complex of JL Thompson's with its cranes and building berths in the background.

A dredger at work in the River Wear. For hundreds of years there has been a constant battle with the elements by those who want to use the river for commercial use. The river has been widened, deepened and protected with piers to ensure that ships can safely come and go. Behind is the old Wearmouth Bridge which was replaced by the present bridge in the late 1920s.

A number of vessels on the Wear in the 1960s including a ship on the berth and another at the fitting-out quay of JL Thompson's.

Shipbuilding in the Nineteenth Century

The closure of the shipyards on the Wear in the 1980s ended centuries of shipbuilding in Sunderland. A document dated back to 1346 stated Thomas Menvill was a shipbuilder at Hendon in Sunderland who paid a rent of two shillings a year to the bishop. Rain's Eye Plan of 1790 shows a number of ships being built on the Monkwearmouth Shore. This early map of Sunderland also depicts industries associated to shipbuilding at this time – sail makers, block yards, rope makers and timber yards. The nineteenth century was the period when Sunderland made a major impact on the shipbuilding world. By the 1850s there were over seventy shipbuilders in the town.

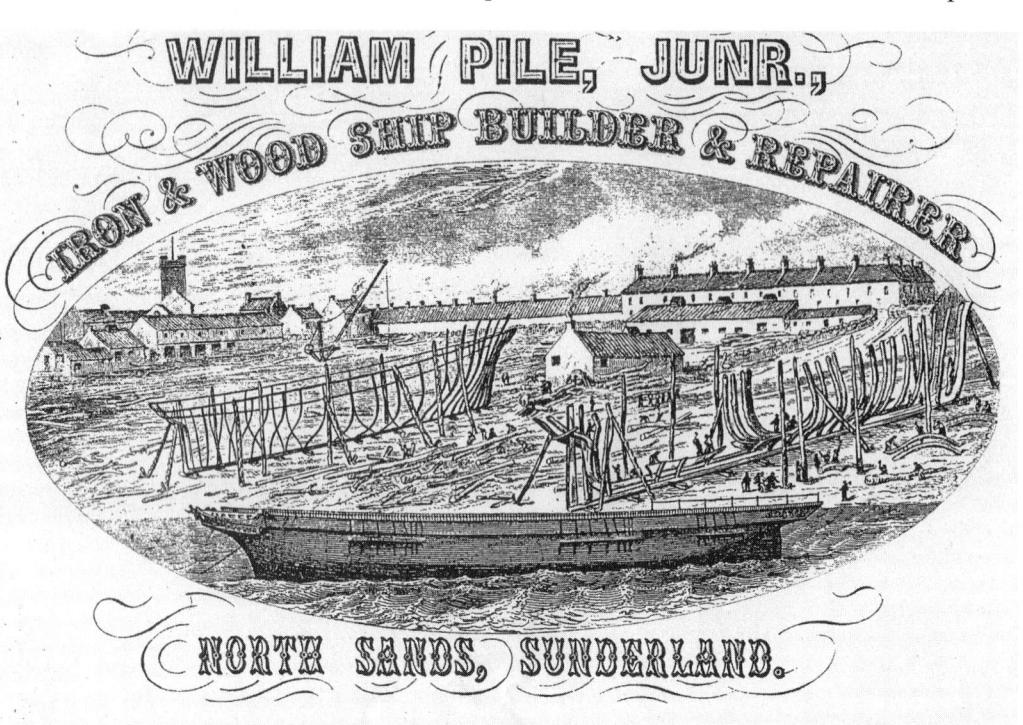

An advertisement for the North Sands yard of William Pile Jnr from *Marwood's Maritime Directory* of 1854. This was a period when iron shipbuilding was replacing wood on the Wear and Pile's yard was turning out both types of vessel. At this time Pile was the most famous shipbuilder in Sunderland. However, his death at the age of only 50 in 1873 was to signal the end of his shipyard. In *Where Ships Are Born* Pile was described as the 'greatest ship designer of his age, but no business man. Costs mattered little to Pile; his only thought was to produce a good ship regardless of profit to himself. That is why he left no fortune, and the stock had to be sold off to meet his creditors.'

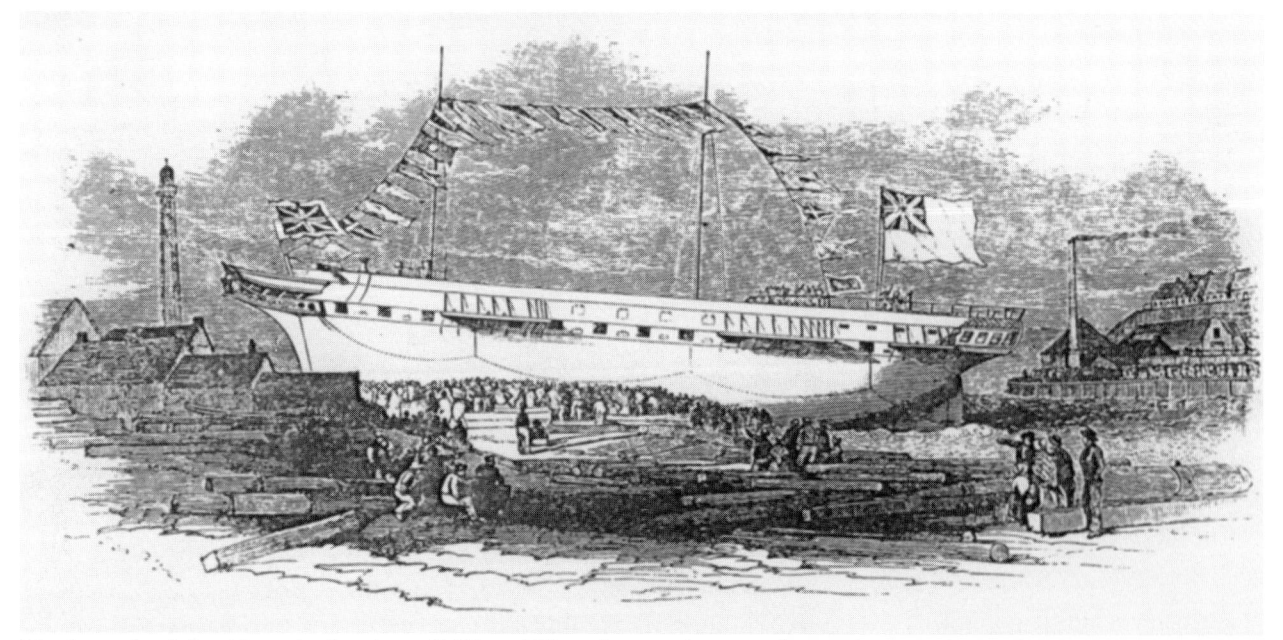

The launch of the *Chowringhee* from William Pile's shipyard at North Sands on 3rd March 1851. It was built for the East India trade and cost owner John Hay of Sunderland £16,000. No expense was spared and the ship had elegant staircases and cabins with skylights. The ship's figure-head featured a man killing a tiger. The commander of the *Chowringhee* was Captain J. Brown of Sunderland.

Sunderland Shipbuilders in 1851

Marwood's Maritime Directory of 1851 gave a list of shipbuilders in Sunderland.

Abbay, Wm. Richard	Ayre's Quay	Hall, G.W. & W.J.	Bridge Dock Yd	Ratcliffe & Spence	North Dock
Alcock, John Thomas	Low Street	Hardie, James	Southwick	Rawson & Watson	North Dock
Austin & Mills	Southwick	Harkess, William	North Sands	Reed, William	Coxgreen
Austin, Samuel Peter	B/mouth Panns	Haswell, J.	North Hylton	Robinson, John & Jas	Deptford
Barkes, John	Wreath Quay	Havelock & Robson	North Dock	Robson, Thomas	Claxheugh
Bainbridge, George	Hylton	Hodgson & Gardiner	North Hylton	Rodgerson, John	South Hylton
Bailey, E.	Ayre's Quay	Hutchinson, John	B/mouth Panns	Smith, John	Pallion
Barker, G.	North Sands	Hutchinson, R & W.	B/mouth Panns	Spowers, Wm & Co	South Hylton
Booth & Blakelock	North Sands	Hutchinson, Ralph	North Quay	Stonehouse, Thomas	Ravenswheel
Briggs, W.	Pallion	Laing, James	Deptford	Stoddart, Matthew	Southwick
Brown, E.	North Hylton	Lister & Bartram	North Hylton	Stothard, Newby	Pallion
Buchannan & Gibson	Ayre's Quay	Lightfoot, Thomas	Hylton Dene	Sykes & Co	Coxgreen
Byrers, Brothers	Strand	Leithead, Arrow	Pallion	Taylor & Son	South Hylton
Carr, William	South Hylton	Leithead, Andrew	Low Southwick	Thompson, R. & Sons	North Sands
Carr, Hylton	North Hylton	Murray, John, J. & P.	North Dock	Tiffin, T. Jnr & Benj	Glasshouse Reach
Candlish, John & R.	Southwick	Naizby, William	Ford Dock Yard	Todd & Brown	North Hylton
Chilton, Wilson	High Southwick	Pearson, Wm Henry	Ayre's Quay	Wallace, William	Glasshouse Reach
Clarke, M.	Southwick	Petrie, William	Southwick	Watson, John	Pallion
Crown, John	Southwick	Peverley & Charlton	South Dock	Watson, Robert Y.	Pallion
Crown, W.	Southwick	Pile, James	North Sands	Wilkinson, Richard	Pallion
Douglas, D.	South Hylton	Pile, John	North Shore	Wilkinson, William	Deptford
Forrest & Jackson	Quarry Hole, Hylton	Pile, William Jnr	North Shore	Worthy, George	Southwick
		Potts, Edward	North Quay	Worthy, William	Dobson's Lime Kiln
Gales, Lawson	South Hylton	Potts, R.H. & Bros	Low Street		

Already shipbuilding at this time were Austin, Bartram, Laing and Thompson.

The barque *Zehlima* on the stocks of Robert Thompson's Southwick yard. The 475 ton vessel was launched on 5th May 1860. The *Zehlima* carried coal to the River Plate and returned from South America with animal hides. Robert Thompson Jnr left the family firm to start shipbuilding at Southwick in 1854. He took over the old building and repair yard of John Candlish. (*Courtesy of Sunderland Museum and Winter Gardens – Tyne and Wear Museums*)

The Hudson Dock at the end of the nineteenth century showing sailing ships alongside steamers.

SMITH & STEVENSON,

CHAIN-CABLE AND ANCHOR MANUFACTURERS,

SHIP AND WHITE SMITHS,

DEALERS IN

HEARTH STOVES, PATENT WINCHES, &c.,

IRONMONGERS, TINNERS, AND BRAZIERS,

CANVAS MANUFACTURERS,

SAIL MAKERS,

BLOCK AND MAST MAKERS,

COOPERS,

AND GENERAL MERCHANTS,

WEAR STREET,

MONKWEARMOUTH, SUNDERLAND.

Above: Another scene showing sailing ships and steamers in Sunderland. The middle of the nineteenth century saw the introduction of iron shipbuilding on the Wear. However, wooden ships continued to be built until 1880 and sailing ships carried on being made for more than another decade. When the end came it was a dark day for the town's canvas and sail makers, rope makers, block makers and timber yards.

Left: Anchors, sails and masts were just a few of the shipbuilding wares manufactured by Monkwearmouth firm Smith and Stevenson in the middle of the nineteenth century. This advert appeared in *Marwood's Maritime Directory* of 1848.

Short's & The Eight Hour Day

On 13th November 1898 *The Times* reported: 'The experiment of an eight hour day has been subjected to tests of the most severe description by a Sunderland shipbuilding firm, Messrs Short Brothers, whose yard is situated on the Wear, in the district known as Pallion. It is now seven years since Messrs Short commenced an eight hour system with a view of reducing hours of labour from fifty-three to forty-eight; and now, at the expiration of that period they express themselves as having every reason to be satisfied with the result. But those who have advocated the general adoption of an eight hour day in shipyards on the plea that more work would then be found for the unemployed, need not look for any confirmation of their theory in the experience of this firm. On the contrary, it has been demonstrated beyond all question at these works that under the new system the men do not lose so much time and really work more hours under the short than they did seven years ago under the longer hours system. Although, of course, the method under which the firm's work is conducted has been known to local people who interest themselves, from a variety of causes, in the matter, yet publicity has not hitherto been given to the subject. Messrs. Short have up to the present deemed it advisable to maintain silence on the point, wishing first of all to give the new departure a thorough and lengthened trial. Briefly put, the experience of Mr J.Y. Short as to the working of the eight hours day is as follows:– His firm have found that instead of the production being less from the apparently shorter hours of work it has, on the contrary, gradually increased since 1891. Messrs, Short took up the system in their belief that they could get the same amount of work out of their employees by a better method than that which then prevailed. Of men working on time wages 15 or 20 per cent lost the first quarter of the day, while the piecemen scarcely ever started before 8.30 under the old method.

The SS *George Fleming* built at Short's in 1897 at the time the yard was operating its pioneering eight hour day.

The men started at 6 o'clock and stopped at 8 for an half hour for breakfast, had another interval of an hour at noon, and the day's work finished at five. The conditions under which the old system was carried out was such that many workmen were physically incapable of maintaining the long hours. It was, in point of fact quite common for a man with 24 shillings a week to lose on an average three quarters per week, simply because he was unable to rise at six o'clock and work full time. Under the system which then obtained in the yard from 15 to 20 per cent of the employees never started until after the first quarter had been lost. Under the 48 hours system, the men start after breakfast at 7.30 and go on with only one break until 5 o'clock, and they are, on the authority of Mr J.Y. Short, able to do more work this way than under the old system, and at the same time more work is got out of the machines, and the results of the eight hours system being an increased out put and a decreased cost. Under the 53 hours, the men did not average anything like 8 hours per day, indeed some of them did not average 5 hours, owing to the time lost. The men work better and more hours under the 48 hours system than under the other while the machinery is also kept running more regularly, and for a greater number of hours. So thoroughly do this Sunderland firm believe in the eight hours day, and so satisfied are they with its working in their yard, that – to use Mr Short's own expression – "They would not go back to the old fashioned way." The seven years' experience, the results of which have thus been indicated, is worthy of the consideration of all employers of labour.'

Life of a Shipyard Worker & His Family A Century Ago

In the early years of the last century a large proportion of Sunderland households depended on men working in the shipyard as breadwinners. There were over 10,000 men employed in shipbuilding and related industries in Sunderland at this time. In 1906 a Board of Trade Report on Working Class Rents, Housing and Retail Prices together with Wage Rates of occupations like shipbuilding was published. Sunderland was one of the principal industrial towns of the United Kingdom that was featured in the Report.

The Report gave the weekly wage of some of the shipyard trades in 1906: Platers – £1 15 shillings and riveters and caulkers – £1 13 shillings. However, these were 'time' rates and as most of the work in the yards was 'piecework' rates this boosted the income considerably. Platers were said to earn between £4 and £8 a week, riveters £2 10s to £4 and caulkers £3 to £4. The weekly wage of holders-up (paid by platers) was given as £1 7s 6d but this was said to be higher than they actually received. This was because they were dependent on platers who tended not to work the full week so holders-up frequently worked only four and half days a week.

> The 1906 Report noted Sunderland had an extensive electric tramway network and 'special workmen's cars are run at a uniform fare of 1d for any distance, and are well filled morning and evening.'

Many men at this time handed over their pay packet to their wife or mother and were given back 'pocket money' to spend on themselves. Men could spend their money in the town's countless public houses or watch their favourites at Roker Park (newly opened in 1898).

Most of the wage would go on food, housing and heating. It was left to the woman of the household to manage the family budget. One source of good cheap food was the numerous Co-op stores in the area which had the added attraction of the 'divi'. This was an era when the Co-operative Society accounted for 'an important share of working-class custom'. Because of its location Sunderland households got the benefit of cheap coal – 9d per hundredweight. Paraffin oil was 8d a gallon at this time. If a woman miscalculated the week's finances or had an unexpected expense before next pay day there was always the pawnshop to tide the family over (there were over fifty pawnbrokers in town at this time).

The 1906 Report stated there were three main types of housing in Sunderland for working men and their families. The first were old tenement buildings mainly in the East End of town. These two or three storey

Residents of a street in Sunderland's East End in the early 1900s.

A view of Harrison's Buildings with the former JL Thompson's shipyard across the river. This was Sunderland's first Council house development but many needed persuading to take up tenancy because of high rents.

buildings had once been the homes of wealthy families but now housed four or more families per building. Residents of these buildings included shipyard labourers and dock workers. The second type of housing was two storey buildings purpose-built for letting as tenements. These had two or three rooms in the ground floor tenement and three to four rooms on the upper floor. The dimensions of rooms in the newer tenements were: sitting-room 13ft 9ins x 13ft, living-room 14ft x 12ft and bedroom 12ft x 8ft. The weekly rents of tenements varied from 1s 6d to 2s for one room to 8s for five rooms. The Report noted that as a rule unskilled workers rarely paid more than 3s 6d to 4s in rent while rent of 7s or more was only paid by foremen and other higher wage earners.

One storey cottages were the third class of housing for the working class in town. These were favoured by skilled craftsmen in the shipyards and were often owner-occupied. These houses consisted of sitting-room, living-room, bedroom and scullery with their own back yard. This type of housing is still a familiar sight in Sunderland today with street after street of cottages in Hendon, Millfield, Pallion and Roker.

In the early 1900s a new form of accommodation for the working man in Sunderland was just being introduced – Council housing. At the turn of the nineteenth century the Council had began to clear the overcrowded tenements in the East End and planned to replace them with the town's first council housing. After delays Harrison's Buildings were finally opened in 1903 with a rent of 4s 6d a week for two-roomed dwellings and 5s 6d for three rooms. Many of the apartments remained unlet and the following year the rent for two rooms was dropped by sixpence a week and the year after a similar reduction was made for three rooms.

Commodity		Predominant Prices in Sunderland in October 1905
Tea	per lb	1s 6d
Potatoes	per 7lbs	2¼d
Bread*	per 4lbs	5½d to 6d
Flour	per 7lbs	8½d to 9d
Milk**	per quart	4d
Sugar (white granulated)	per lb	2d
Eggs	per 16	1s
Cheese (American cheddar)	per lb	7d
Butter	per lb	1s to 1s 3d
Salt	per lb	1s
Bacon (streaky)	per lb	7d to 8d
Beef (silverside)	per lb	8d to 9d
Mutton (leg)	per lb	8d to 9½d
Pork (chops)	per lb	9d

* Most Sunderland households at this time did not buy bread but baked their own.

** Milk was a penny a quart cheaper in the summer months.

Wear shipyards were enjoying a boom time a century ago. The year 1905 broke all records for shipbuilding on the Wear. A total of 95 vessels were built (22 more than 1904) with total output up 95,527 tons on the previous year to 342,797 tons. In the early months of the year although there were orders on the books they were at a low price. In consequence the employers gave notice of decreases in wages and after negotiations the workforce accepted this. By the end of the year the employers agreed to the workers' request for higher wages.

The record output set in 1905 was surpassed the following year. A total of 99 ships (365,951 tons) were built in Sunderland yards. For the second year running Doxford's had the greatest output from a Wear yard with 25 ships (106,068 tons) – a launch every fortnight.

Above: A photograph taken from Wear Garth in the 1960s showing a ship at the Manor Quay with Barclay Court on Dame Dorothy Street in the background.

Left and below: Two views of J.L. Thompson's again looking from the Garths on the southside of the river.

Prior to 1957 workers living in the East End could get the ferry to JL Thompson's and those from Monkwearmouth (Barbary Coasters) could use it to reach Bartram's.

The Coal Trade & Shipbuilding

A brochure produced by the Port of Sunderland in 1929 claimed: 'Sunderland Coals are best.' It went on to describe the coal trade at that time:

'As the principal port in County Durham, Sunderland derives its coal for shipment from the many collieries by which it is surrounded. The earliest mention of coal in the County of Durham was at Bishop Wearmouth in the year 1180, and the first exportation recorded was in 1396. Shipments from the Wear assumed greater proportions in the 17th century, when larger quantities were sent to London … Coals shipped at Sunderland are specially used for gas making; coke making; by-product plants; steam raising; all smithy purposes; household fuel, etc.

Amongst the colliery companies shipping coal at Sunderland, are the following well-known suppliers: Lambton, Hetton & Joicey Collieries, Wearmouth Coal Co, Ryhope Coal Co, South Hetton Coal Co, Londonderry Collieries, Easington Coal Co, Holmside and South Moor Collieries and many more … The volume of the coal shipments from Sunderland can be gauged by the fact that in 1928 they aggregated 5,393,507 tons.'

Crowds gather to cheer the first shipments of coal leaving the new Sunderland Docks in 1850.

Two of Wearside's famous industries on the banks of the River Wear. On the right is Wearmouth Colliery which closed in 1993 and across the river is the former shipyard of Laing's.

The coal staithes in the Hudson Dock North in the 1890s. The steamer is the *Perseverance* launched from Shorts Brothers in 1881. It was built for Freear and Dix of Sunderland for trade with the Baltic and White Sea ports.

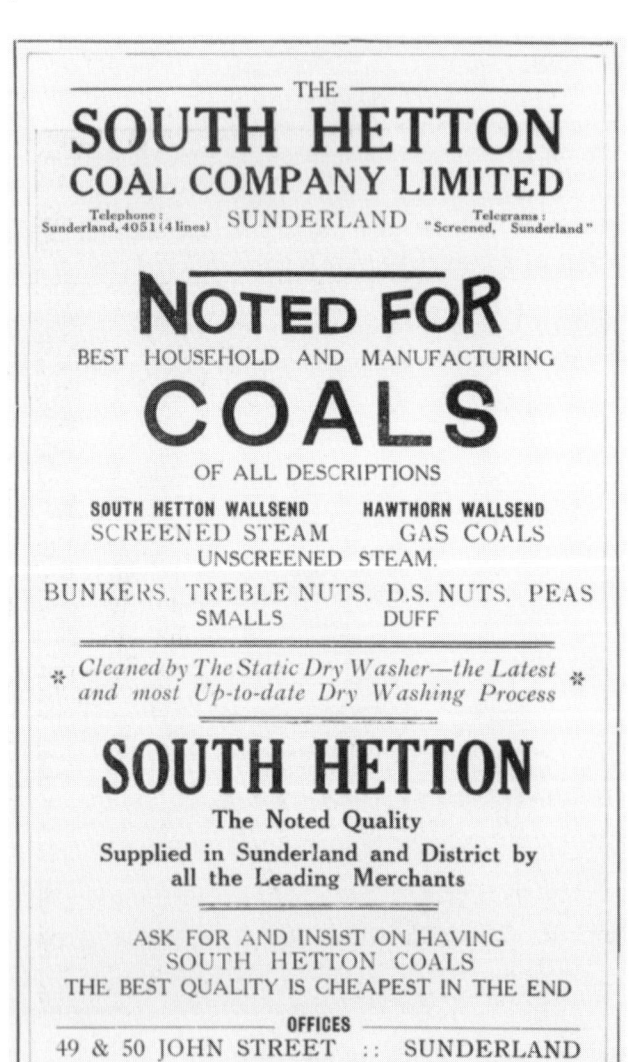

Left: An advert for South Hetton Coal Company which shipped coal out of Sunderland from its collieries at South Hetton and Murton. The company's coal was exported to Sweden and Norway and its gas coal was shipped to London gas companies.

In the early 1930s between five and six million tons of coal was being shipped from Sunderland. The largest exporter was the Lambton, Hetton & Joicey Collieries which alone shipped three million tons of coal annually. This coal went to Germany, France, Denmark, Norway, Sweden, Portugal and Italy. London was also a main destination for this company's steam and gas coal.

After the Second World War the demand for colliers reached new peaks. The launch of the 1,700 ton *Poole Harbour* from John Crown's Strand slipway on 16th December 1948 was the first of ten vessels on order for Coastwise Colliers of London from yards on the Wear.

Between 1946 and 1950 Austin's alone built over twenty colliers, including: *Sir Alexander Kennedy, Brixton, Laverock, Seamew, Seaford, Martin Carl, Poul Carl, Branksome, Coleford, Catford, Pompey Power, Pompey Light, Culville, Auk, Elisabeth Neilson, Goodwood, Samuel Clegg, Polden, Bodmin Moor, Brent Knoll, Wychwood* and *Ardingly*.

Right: The MV *Samuel Clegg* built at Austin's for the North Thames Gas Board and launched on 19th October 1949. The photograph shows a McGregor's Patent Single Steel Hatch Cover. The hatch was 43 feet long and 23 feet broad in the open position and took one minute to open.

A book produced by Austin's in 1954 said that in the early part of the twentieth century: 'There is hardly a fleet of colliers which does not contain some Austin-built vessels. Indeed, some of the more important fleets consist almost entirely of Austin-built ships, and this serves to confirm the statement that the name Austin in the Collier trade is synonymous with that of Rolls Royce in the motor car world.'

The book went on to say: 'Another trade which was pioneered by Austin's was the Thames up-river trade. Sea-borne coal was always cheaper than rail-borne coal and the large gas companies and electric companies were quick to realise this. On the River Thames there were gas and electricity stations well up river and to get to them there were all the London bridges over the river to negotiate. The result was coal from the north had to be loaded into barges and taken up river at, of course, added cost. Austin's got down to this and designed a vessel to carry coal right under all the bridges to the gas and electricity station itself. This entailed a lot of pioneer work in design. The lowest bridge had to be cleared and this meant limitation of height of structure and also draft to suit the river. Funnel, ventilators and masts were hinged and the result was coal delivered right to the gas company's wharf.'

Left: The collier *Benton* being loaded from Nos 1 and 2 coal belt conveyors at the South Docks in the 1920s.

19

First World War

When the First World War broke out in 1918 there were 14 shipyards working in Sunderland. These yards launched almost 200 merchant vessels during the conflict as well as many naval ships.

The book *Where Ships Are Born* gives an approximate record of the merchant vessels built on the Wear in the four years of 1915 to 1918:

	Ships	Gross Tons
Laing's	18	109,924
Doxford's	16	94,298
JL Thompson's	17	91,486
Short's	17	86,391
Priestman's	15	63,627
Pickersgill's	12	54,715
Blumer's	14	48,456
Sunderland Shipbuilding	11	42,979
Bartram's	12	41,658
R. Thompson's	10	31,702
Austin's	13	28,979
Osbourne Graham's	12	26,442
Crown's	8	14,591
Swan Hunter's	No Record	

A large crowd cheer George V and Queen Mary as they leave Doxford's on 15th June 1917. The Royal party also toured Laing's, JL Thompson's, Pickersgill's and John Crown's during their visit to Sunderland.

HMS *Mantis* ready for a broadside launch from Sunderland Shipbuilding Company yard on 14th September 1915. This yard occupied a site in the South Dock formerly owned by John Haswell. It was known as the 'Limited' yard but it did not survive the post-war slump and closed in the 1920s. *(Courtesy of Sunderland Museum and Winter Gardens – Tyne and Wear Museums)*

Two views of HMS *Opal* before its launch from Doxford's on 11th September 1915. This was one of twenty-one torpedo boat destroyers Doxford's built during the First World War.

Doxford Men At The Munitions Court

At a Munitions Court held at Newcastle on 13th October 1915 four boilermakers were charged with having played cards at 5.30 in the morning of 25th September 1915 at William Doxford's works. The court disclosed the average earnings of each man over a six week period – Edward W. Bewes £2 18s 6d, E.E. Butchart £3 10s 6d, Fred Cockerell £3 15s 7d and Fred Wolfe £2 7s 9d. All the men pleaded guilty to the charge and each was fined 30 shillings.

These Munition Courts were held all round the country. At Manchester Munitions Court also held in October 1915 Manchester City footballer Horace Barnes was fined £2 for leaving work on an automatic munition machine on Saturday 9th October. He had asked permission to turn out in a match but was refused and went absent to play.

Right: The *Capelcastle*, in its wartime colours, built at Robert Thompson's in 1917.

In the last year of the First World War the Egis yard was started at Pallion. It was formed from the initial letters of the names of the yard's founders – Sir John Ellerman (shipbuilder), Sir William Gray (West Hartlepool shipbuilder), Lord Inchcape (P & O Line) and F.C. Strick. The yard up river from Short's at Pallion later became known as Sir William Gray's but it did not survive the Depression years.

The Depression Years

Over the years there had always been booms and slumps in shipbuilding – in time of war output soared and was usually followed by a post-war drought. In the 1920s the Wear order books dried up and in 1923 JL Thompson's and Bartram's built no ships. Doxford's was suffering even more and closed down from September 1924 until April 1927. In 1925 James Marr set up the Silver Line and placed an order for six cargo ships with Laing's and JL Thompson's, building three each and all with Doxford engines. Marr also built a graving dock at Greenwell's with Sunderland Forge supplying the electrical machinery for the project.

The hard times experienced in Sunderland during the 1920s was followed in the next decade by the Great Depression. Only seven ships were launched from Wear yards in 1931. Two of these were 500 ton Wear Hoppers No 36 and No 37 and the rest colliers. Two of these vessels had to be completed for different owners. The following year was even worse with only two ships built – the colliers *Tyndall* and *John Hopkinson* for Austin's. In 1933 five ships were built in Sunderland yards and eight vessels in each of the following two years.

James Marr, who took positive action in 1925 to create work for his yards.

Silver Line ships continued to be built at Sunderland after the Depression. The *Silverbriar* (above) and the *Silverlaurel* (right) were both built on the Wear in the post-war period.

22

Boots For The Bairns In 1926

The shipbuilding slump on the Wear in 1926 (only seven ships built) contributed to a time of great hardship in the town. The Mayor's Fund set a target of £2,000 to supply children in Sunderland with footwear for the winter months. It cost an average of seven shillings to provide a boy or girl with boots and stockings. Despite the problems in the shipyards Austin's donated £10 10s (enough for 30 children not to go barefoot). By Christmas Eve 1926 the Fund had reached £1,481 5s 3d.

At the height of the Depression some men still had faith in shipbuilding on the Wear and placed orders. Sir Joseph Isherwood placed orders for three ships of a new design he hoped would bring tramp steamers 'back into their own.' The *Arcwear*, first of these, was launched from Short's on 1st November 1933.

Doxford's were forced to close their yard again in 1931 but at this time the company set about designing a cost-saving tramp ship. The Doxford Economy Ship would cost £100,000 but had low operational costs and later owners could take advantage of the government's Scrap & Build Scheme (introduced in 1935). The first in the series of ships was the *Sutherland* launched on 6th December 1934. At the naming ceremony the owner, Sir Arthur Sutherland, said: 'It is nothing short of a tragedy that this fine yard should have been standing idle for four years without a launch. I am more than pleased that, as a result of these orders, there are now 1,000 men at work.' The owner returned to Sunderland on 24th March 1936 for the launch of the *Peebles*. On this occasion he declared he was 'happy to hear the clanging of the shipyard hammers in the yard and to know that 3,000 men are working there. It was a great change compared with 15 months ago when the first of the six vessels ordered from Messrs Doxford's was launched.'

The *Arcwear* which helped Short's continue to work in the worst days of the Depression.

The *Sutherland* – the first of the Doxford Economy Ship.

Austin's Repair Work

In 1934 Austin's built five colliers – *Corfirth*, *Corfleet*, *Wychwood*, *Corfell* and *Hawkwood* – but also did repair work on 360 vessels. Fifty of these ships were worked on the pontoon or in dry dock.

Second World War

The shipyards of Sunderland played a crucial role in the war effort and a record number of ships, vital for the survival of the country, were built. Doxford's was the busiest yard and launched 75 merchant vessels. This was 32 more than the second yard which was JL Thompson's. In 1942 Thompson's broke a 36 year old production record when it launched ten vessels with a gross tonnage of 71,961. The following year the shipyard suffered the fate of many wartime industries – it was targeted by the Luftwaffe. During two air raids in May 1943 the yard suffered severe damage and a ship was sunk in the River Wear. The yard was immediately rebuilt and still managed to launch five ships that year.

Laing's also suffered bomb damage when, during a day time raid in 1940, four men were killed after five bombs fell on the yard at lunch time. The casualties and damage could have been far worse as three of the bombs failed to explode.

Despite air raids, lack of resources and skilled men, between September 1939 and September 1944, Sunderland shipyards built 245 1/2 ships with a gross tonnage of 1,503,239. The 'half a ship' was a new fore end for an oil tanker which had been damaged.

The Duke of Kent meets some 'older' workers on his visit to JL Thompson's in June 1941. With many workers in the forces during the war, veteran shipyard men worked alongside boys and women in the yards. Even with the lack of manpower, production records were broken on the Wear.

John Crown's Wartime Contribution

During the Second World War John Crown's yard at Monkwearmouth built a number of corvettes for the Admiralty. Among these were the *Heliotrope, Hollyhock, Burdock, Campion, Godetia, Bugloss* and *Farnham Castle*. The small yard also completed the frigate *Ettrick* and two trawlers.

When the war ended Crown's yard did not have much time to get back to peacetime production – in 1946 it was bought out by JL Thompson's. Crown's location at North Sands must have been one of the prime motives in JL Thompson's purchase of the yard.

Left: An advert for John Crown's yard at the end of the war when it was returning to peacetime work.

Clementine Churchill watches 19-year-old apprentice welder Albert Adams demonstrate his skills. The Prime Minister's wife was paying a wartime visit to Bartram's yard in April 1941. *(Courtesy of Sunderland Museum and Winter Gardens – Tyne and Wear Museums)*

A Shipbuilder's War

R. Cyril Thompson, managing director of JL Thompson's, had an interesting wartime career. In 1940 he travelled to America with plans for one of JL Thompson's vessels to be built in US and Canadian shipyards. Mass construction methods were applied to this standard design and thousands of 'Liberty Ships' were turned out from the North American yards. These ships were vital to the war effort replacing ships lost to U-boats. Between 1942 and 1943 the United States alone built 2,710 Liberty ships amounting to 20 million tons

On Thompson's return voyage from America his ship was torpedoed but he survived and was rescued by a tramp steamer. In 1942 he was the driving force behind the building of a new yard on the former Swan Hunter's site in Southwick. The yard was derelict when took over but within a year it was rebuilt and launched its first ship.

He left the family firm in 1944 to serve in the RAF as a flight engineer and saw active service in Italy before returning to the shipyard in 1945.

Cyril Thompson was awarded a CBE in 1941 for his contribution to the war effort.

R. Cyril Thompson

Age of the Greek Tycoons

In 1949 the Greek merchant fleet was the ninth largest in the world – thirty years later it was the largest and Sunderland shipyards played their part in this meteoric rise. In the 1950s, '60s and '70s Greek shipowners and their agents placed orders for over one hundred ships with Wear yards. Names like Nicholas Livanos, Chandris Group, Lyras Brothers, Embiricos, Fafalios and Rethymnis and Kulukundis regularly attended launch ceremonies on Wearside. From 1957 Greek-born Basil Mavroleon headed a consortium that even owned one yard – Austin & Pickersgill's – which in turn built many ships for Greek owners. Even the three most famous Greek shipping tycoons – Aristotle Onassis, Stavros Niarchos and Stavros Livanos – placed orders with Sunderland shipyards.

Although the boom years for Greek shipbuilding was the post-war period vessels had been built for Greek owners as far back as the nineteenth century. The Embiricos family had the steel screw steamer *Leonidas* launched from Short's on 4th November 1896. On 17th May 1920 the steamer *Eugenie S. Embiricos* was launched from Short's. The *Sunderland Daily Echo* reported on the living quarters on the *Eugenie S. Embiricos*: 'Accommodation for the owner with dining salon etc is arranged in a house on the shelter deck; for the master and Marconi (radio) apparatus and operators in the house on the top saloon house; with chart and wheelhouse above; for the officers and engineers in the houses abreast of and after end of the engine casing; and for the crew and petty officers at the after end of the shelter deck.' Wear yards continued to build ships for the family into the twentieth century. Other ships constructed on the Wear for Greek owners included the *Iossifoglu* built at Robert Thompson's for Mr S. Iossifoglu of Athens. The cargo steamer was launched from the Southwick yard on 20th February 1913. Robert Thompson's also built the grain carrier *George M. Livanos* for the Livanos Brothers. The naming ceremony for the 7,200 ton single screw steamer on 4th April 1928 was performed by Mrs Stavros Livanos. Her husband said that the launch had been very successful and he hoped the ship would be successful. In 1930 William Gray's shipyard built two ships for Greek owners. The *Atthis* for Rethymnis & Kulukundis went down the Pallion yard's slipway on 3rd April. The naming ceremony was performed by Helen Kulukundis and her husband Manuel recalled how Sir William Gray's firm had built many good ships for Greek owners. The following month the *Thetis*, built for Hadjilias of Athens, was to be the last ship ever built at William Gray's yard. After the launch of the 10,000 cargo steamer *Elias G. Kulukundis*, from Short's on 18th March 1938, Captain Nicholas Kulukundis, superintendent and director of Rethymnis & Kulukundis, said he believed the North East coast was now ahead of the Clyde yards when it came to building economical cargo vessels. After the *Kassos* was launched from Doxford's on 1st June 1939 it became the first motor vessel to fly the Greek flag. At the launch of the *Kassos* Manuel Kulukundis stated his company had seven ships built on the Wear the previous year and said: 'We are very happy to deal with you here, because we always receive such a fine welcome.'

Many of the companies of this early period were to feature in the phenomenal rise of the Greek merchant fleet in the post-war years. When Doxford's launched the 12,600 ton *Stamatios G. Embiricos* on 9th July 1956 the owner Mr S.G. Embiricos recalled that it was 36 years since his company last had a ship built by Doxford's – *Assimina M. Embiricos*.

Rethymnis & Kulukundis had been formed by five Kulukundis brothers, members of the Rethymnis family and the Mavroleon brothers (including Basil

The 12,500 ton Dona Katerina. The launch of the ship from Doxford's on 26th July 1957 had to be cancelled because of high winds. The naming ceremony went ahead as scheduled, performed by Mrs S.D. Sarandis, the great-aunt of Peter and Michael Chandris. The launch party was disappointed not to see the Dona Katerina go into the water the following day.

Miss Chandris launched from Doxford's on 11th May 1959. The Chandris Group went on to control one of the largest merchant fleets in the world.

who was to later own Austin & Pickersgill's). The company and its various subsidiaries had scores of vessels built by Sunderland yards. At the launch of the *Aghia Marina* from Doxford's on 22nd March 1954 Captain Rethymnis, a principal of the managers, said he was confident the ship would be as successful as the *Kassos* built by the same firm fifteen years before. The ship was all-welded which saved 350 tons of steel in construction and so needed a lower powered engine. This in turn meant the vessel used less fuel than a riveted ship – a saving of 2$^{1}/_{4}$ tons of fuel per day. Another of the differences between the *Kassos* and *Aghia Marina* was that the new ship would not be flying the Greek flag. Captain Rethymnis said this was only a temporary measure because there were differences between Greek shipowners and the Greek government at this time.

After working together in the 1920s the Livanos brothers went their separate ways but Nicholas G. Livanos went on to have a long association with Wear yards. After the launch of the *Pearl Clipper* from Doxford's on 30th December 1959 another ten vessels were built for N.G. Livanos in the following decade by the Doxford Group.

New Greek shipowners like the Chandris Group Lyras Brothers, Fafalios and Papalios (Aegis Shipping) also kept the order books of the Wear yards full at this time.

In 1954 the *Charlton Venus* was the first of 11 ships Doxford's built for Chandris over the next fifteen years. At the launch of the *Dona Ourania* on 2nd November 1955 the Chandris Group heard of

The 16,500 ton motor ship Pearl Island ready for launch from Doxford's on 24th June 1964. This was one of 11 vessels built for N.G. Livanos in the 1960s.

The Doxford-built 20,000 ton bulk carrier Sinsmetal. The international nature of the shipping industry was demonstrated in the connections of this vessel. Mrs G.S. Gilder travelled to Sunderland from Australia to name the ship on 20th November 1968. Her husband was chairman of Alfred G. Sims Limited of Sydney. The ship was built for the Greek Chandris Group based in London who acted as general agents for Zante Navegacion of Panama.

the work of Sunderland League of Hospital Friends and gave a cheque to provide curtained cubicles for patients' privacy in one of the wards of the General Hospital.

After the launch of the *Federal Lakes* from Deptford (Laing's) yard on 20th January 1969 the chairman of the Doxford & Sunderland Group, C.E. Wrangham, stated: 'Over the past 30 years shipyards now in the Doxford Group had received orders for 45 Greek ships totalling 865,000 tons dwt and 11 of these, totalling 176,000 dwt, for owners of the *Federal Lakes*.' He went on to add: 'Every Greek-owned ship completed in the past two years in Britain has been constructed on the River Wear. This totalled 347,000 tons dwt of which 200,000 tons had come from the Doxford Group.'

In the late 1960s and early '70s Fafalios Ltd and the Lyras Brothers placed orders for 11 vessels with the Doxford Group. These included the *Iktinos*, *Iason*, *Feax*, *Finix*, *Faethon*, *John Lyras* and *Flisvos*.

Many of the Greek shipowners were

Stavros Niarchos and wife Eugenie with youngest son Constantine. The Niarchos Group had the World Explorer launched from Short's in 1961.

related and family ties linked three of the most powerful shipping dynasties. Not only was Stavros Livanos the brother of Nicholas Livanos but also father-in-law to Aristotle Onassis and Stavros Niarchos. Stavros Livanos' daughter Eugenie married Niarchos and her sister Athina married Onassis. When Eugenie died, Athina by this time divorced from Onassis, married her sister's widower. The sisters bore children who inherited the wealth of Onassis and Niarchos but it was their brother, Georges, who took control of Stavros Livanos' merchant fleet.

Onassis and Niarchos epitomized the playboy image of Greek tycoons. Apart from marrying the same woman both men made their fortunes by building up their fleets to take advantage of the increase in oil trade in the post-war period.

In January 1957 Short's announced a multi-million pound order for two ships for Stavros Niarchos' company. Later the 20,000 ton *World Explorer* was built at Short's for the Niarchos Group. The launch had to be postponed because of bad weather before the ship finally went into the water in the early hours of 25th October 1961 in darkness.

One of Aristotle Onassis' companies (Dekos Trading SA of Panama) placed an order for four SD 14s in November 1966. The joint managing director of Bartram's, Cecil McFetrich, declared: 'We are delighted to be able to announce our first order, for the SD 14, particularly in view of the fact that the owners are members of

The Doxford-built 16,000 ton Marigo R. The general cargo ship was launched on 23rd September 1968 with Elli Rethymnis performing the naming ceremony. The Marigo R was launched 29 years after Doxford's completed the Kassos for the same Greek owners.

28

the Onassis Group. This will be the first occasion on which the Group has built new tonnage in Great Britain and we regard it as a great compliment which we shall do our best to justify.' Unfortunately the order was cancelled the following year. Ironically problems over credit facilities for a company owned by one of the richest men in the world caused the cancellation of the order. Greek owners took over the cancelled order with Aegis Shipping having the *Mimis N. Papalios* launched on 1st December 1967 followed by the *George N. Papalios* on 29th February 1968. A third ship for the Onassis Group was taken over by Alafouzos Shipping of Piraeus and went down Bartram's slipway as the *Capetan Giannis* on 9th July 1968. Aegis were also willing to take up the option on the fourth vessel but it was agreed this should be built at Hellenic Shipyards in Skaramanga, Greece under licence. This was one of the first orders under the licence agreement which allowed shipyards in Greece, Brazil, Argentina, Scotland and Smith Dock in Middlesbrough to build SD 14s.

In 1957 Austin & Pickersgill's was taken over by a consortium led by London & Overseas Freighters. London & Overseas Freighters was in turn part of the Rethymnis & Kulukundis/Mavroleon Brothers group with Basil Mavroleon as its colourful figurehead. He is remembered for having a luxury yacht built at A&P's during a slack period at the yard. In 1961 the £400,000

Aristotle Onassis at his wedding to Jacqueline Kennedy in 1968. Despite Onassis' vast wealth the previous year an order from one of his companies for four SD 14s from Bartram's had to be cancelled because of difficulties over credit guarantees.

After the launch of the 47,000 ton bulk carrier G.M. Livanos on 26th April 1968 the managing director of Sunderland Shipbuilders, Victor Thompson, declared workers at JL Thompson's North Sands shipyard were the best in the world.

Radiant II was launched from the Wear Dockyard. The following year the *Radiant II* was anchored in Stockholm harbour during a British Trade Fair in the Swedish capital to advertise the Wear shipping industry.

Two more luxury yachts – *Suniper* and *Bobbina* – were built at the yard for London businessmen.

When the SD 14 was developed by A&P's to replace the Liberty ship in the 1960s Basil Mavroleon led the way. His company placed orders for the first two SD 14s. When the *Nicola* was handed over in 1968 it sailed to London Docks to be inspected by prospective Greek

Doxford's

Doxford's made their home in Pallion for almost 150 years. However, William Doxford, who founded the firm in 1840, started building ships a lot further up river at Cox Green. He moved his shipbuilding operation to Pallion in 1857 but it was not until 1870 that the company bought the land that was to be their home for over hundred years. The family firm quickly developed the site and by the early 1900s, when the East Yard was built, Doxford's was one of the greatest shipyards in the world. The extra capacity of the East Yard, with the most up-to-date equipment of its time, helped earn Doxford's the shipbuilding 'blue riband' in 1905 and 1907 with the highest production of any yard in the world. The six berths built 86,632 tons in 1905 and 92,000 tons in 1907. In 1906, when Doxford's failed to win the blue riband, the yard's output was 106,050 tons which represented a ship every two weeks. That year the Wear produced a total of 365,951 tons which was 18.5% of the country's shipbuilding output.

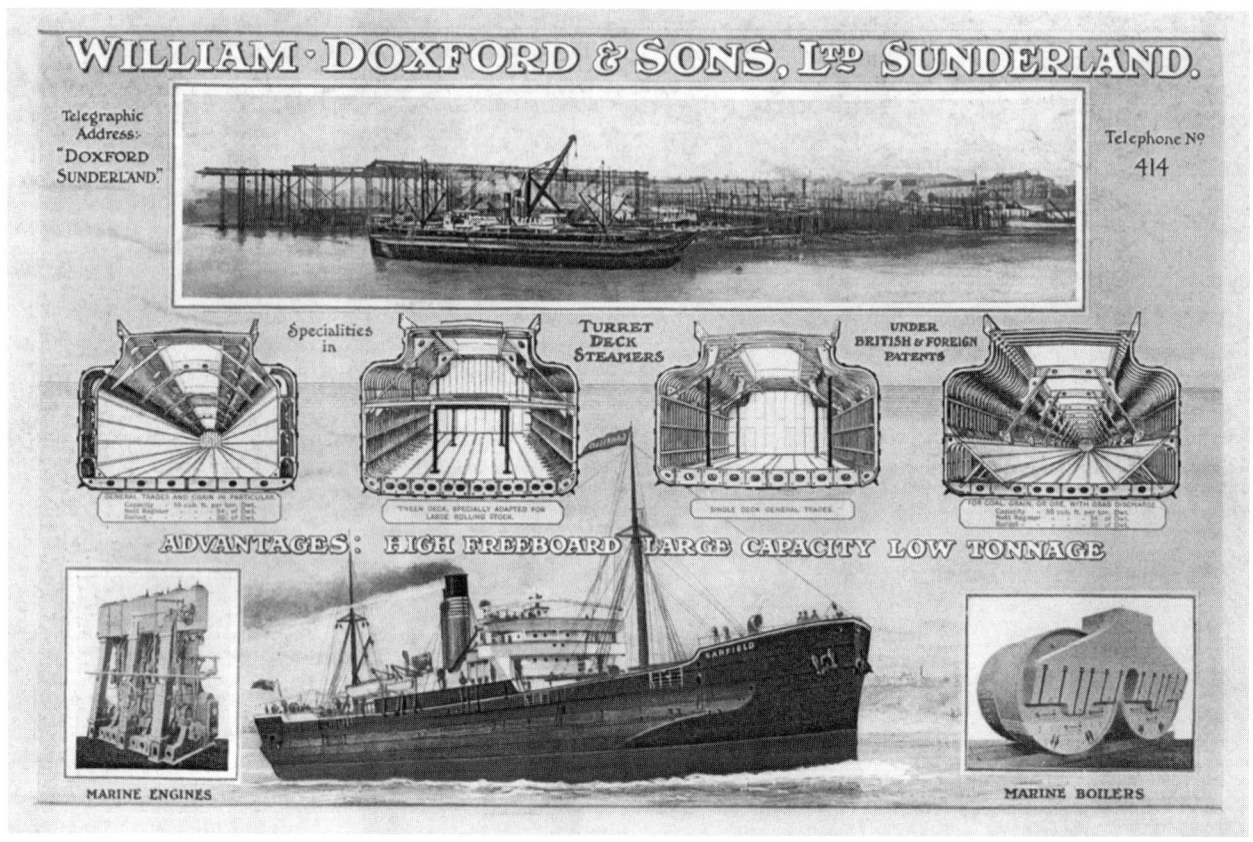

An advert for Doxford's after the yard was rebuilt in the early 1900s.

Left: The *Grangeberg* was one of Doxford's world famous turret ships. The iron ore carrier was launched from the Pallion yard on 14th March 1903.

An aerial view of the thriving industry that was once in the heart of Sunderland around 1950. On the right of the river (the Pallion side) are the towering berths of Doxford's. On the left (the Southwick side) is the smaller yard of Pickersgill's.

Doxford's blacksmiths and strikers in 1914. This was a trade that declined in the shipyards as the century progressed. In 1965 there were only 67 blacksmiths in all of the yards on the Wear.

Left: A view of the *Aztec* under construction at Doxford's. It shows the cylindrical tanks of the oil tanker before framing. The 5,665 ton *Aztec* was launched from the Pallion yard on 9th April 1914.

A Lifetime at Doxford's

When 70 year old Billy Graham retired from the plumbers' shop at Doxford's Pallion yard on 20th October 1967 he had been with the firm for an amazing 55 years. His working life at Doxford's was only broken by four years service in the Durham Light Infantry in France and Belgium during the First World War. On leaving Doxford's, Billy of Ford Estate, was presented with a watch from his workmates and a wallet of notes from the company.

The 'Elephant' or crane tank *Millfield* at Doxford's. It was built in 1906 by Hawthorn & Leslie of Newcastle and was scrapped in 1938. Other locomotives at the yard at this time were the *Pallion, Roker, Hendon* and *Southwick*, which survived until the early 1970s when the yard was modernized.

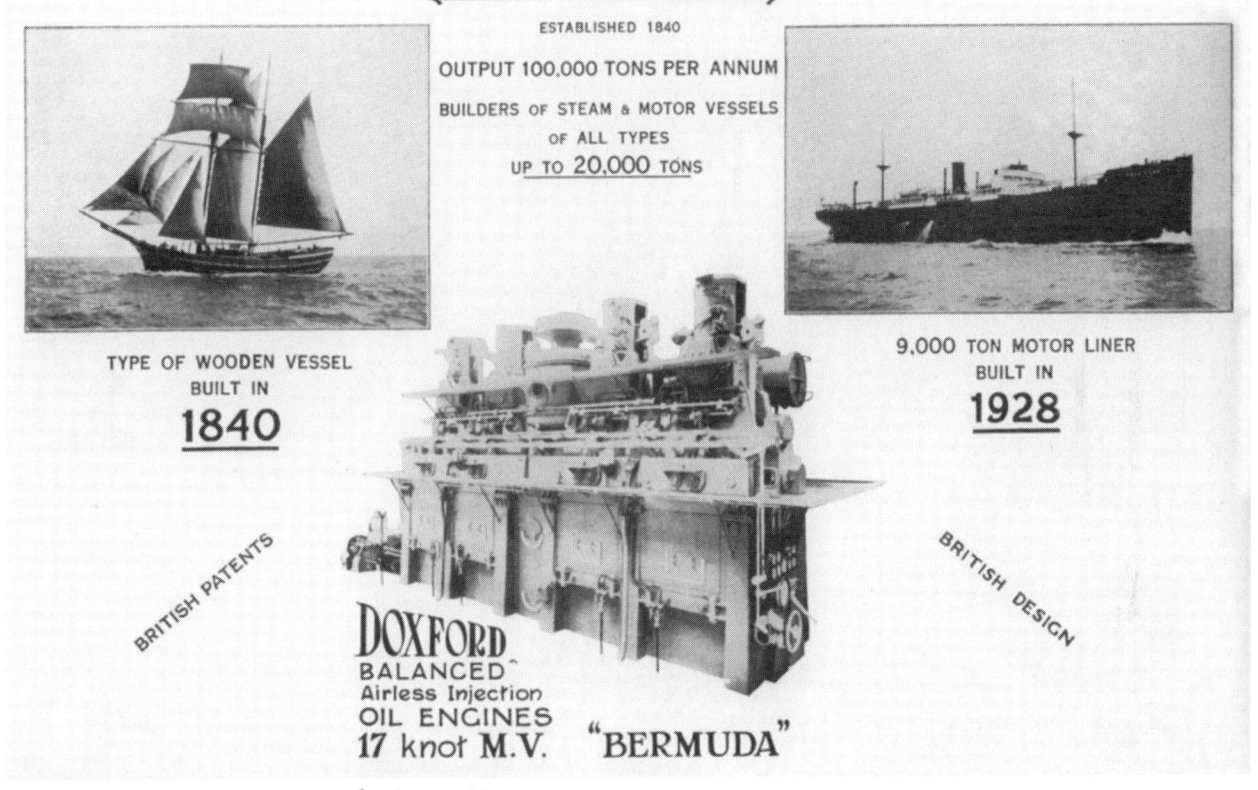

An advert for Doxford's from the late 1920s.

A cargo vessel on the berths at Doxford's in the late 1940s.

The *Firbank* was the first of an order of eight ships Doxford's built for the Bank Line. The 10,450 ton motor ship was launched on 22nd October 1956.

A view of the old East Yard's berths before they made way for the covered building hall. When the East Yard was built in the early 1900s it was one of the most modern shipyards in the world. By the late 1960s the advance in shipbuilding technology had left these facilities lagging behind.

When the *Sylvafield* was launched on 15th April 1953 it was the largest ship built at Doxford's up to that time. The 550ft 16,500 ton motor tanker was built for Hunting & Son of Newcastle.

After the Second World War, Doxford's redeveloped the yard and built massive prefabrication sheds while reducing the number of berths from six to three. The next major reconstruction at the yard once again put Doxford's at the forefront of shipbuilding technology. In 1972 the old yard at Pallion was demolished and in its place was built one of the most advanced shipbuilding centres in the world with a covered hall and state of the art facilities. The new yard was officially opened on 8th April 1976 and at that time was the largest totally enclosed shipyard in the world.

Although shipbuilding came to an end in Sunderland in the late 1980s, the Doxford's yard still remains as a reminder of the river's industrial heritage.

The outdoor steel stockyard next to Doxford's covered yard at Pallion. This was one of the few parts of the new 'ship factory' that was not protected from the elements.

The computer room at the Sunderland Shipbuilders Group headquarters at Pallion. These early computers show how advanced shipbuilding was on the Wear in the 1970s.

The roller conveyor at No 2 Bay at Doxford's yard in the 1970s. The man in the top left of the picture is operating the crane which transferred the plates to the multi-head profile-cutting machines.

Left: The assembly bays at Doxford's Pallion yard in the 1970s. This was a stage in the 'flow-line production process' where the latest construction and welding methods were used.

Right: The drawing offices of Sunderland Shipbuilders next to the covered yard at Pallion.

Below: A view of the huge indoor building dock at Doxford's with Queen Alexandra Bridge in the background. These magnificent facilities should have seen Sunderland at the forefront of world ship construction well into the twenty-first century. However, their shipbuilding life was to be less than twenty years.

Doxford's Engines

Above: An engine being stripped down after testing in Doxford's Engine Works in the mid 1970s. The works was founded in 1878 and quickly established itself as one of the leading engine manufacturers in the world. In 1901 a fire destroyed the old works but within three months the site was rebuilt with more modern equipment installed. The business quickly expanded and by the 1930s ninety per cent of the world's diesel engines were built or designed by Doxford's. In 1945 1,500 men worked in the engine shop, while 2,500 were employed in shipbuilding at Doxford's. In the boom years after the Second World War the Doxford Engine was also manufactured under licence by fourteen other firms including ones in America, Canada and Holland. However, competition from overseas took its toll on the famous works and they went into a steady decline until closure in 1984 with the loss of 206 jobs.

Top right: A crankshaft in Doxford's Engine Works in the mid 1970s.

Right: A 76J9 Doxford Marine Oil Engine on the test bed at the Engine Works in the 1960s. As in the other pictures the men working on these engines give an idea of the gigantic scale of these mechanical marvels.

JL Thompson's

The Thompson dynasty began with Robert Thompson who started building ships on the Wear in the early nineteenth century. By 1846 Robert and his three sons established a yard at North Sands which was to be the firm's home for over 130 years. In 1860 Robert died and the following year only Joseph Lowes Thompson was still with the company. Joseph's brother Robert Jnr had left the firm in 1854 to set up his own shipyard at Southwick. This company became Robert Thompson and Sons and were known for their broadside launches. This branch of the Thompson shipbuilding tree came to an end when the yard closed in 1933. Meanwhile, JL Thompson's survived the 'hungry thirties' and went on to make a valuable contribution to the Second World War.

In the 1960s Thompson's spent millions of pounds to expand their capacity which allowed the firm to build ships up to 150,000 tons. In 1962 the tanker the *British Cavalier* was launched from JL Thompson's and at that time was the biggest vessel ever launched on the Wear. Further records were broken as the yard continued to build bigger and bigger ships throughout the 1960s and '70s. However, the end of the decade saw the yard mothballed until 1986 when the giant crane ship, *Challenger*, was built. This became the last vessel built at the yard which is now the site of the Sunderland University campus.

Robert Thompson Snr

Right: Joseph L. Thompson's shipyard around 1898. A Guide to Sunderland from 1898 gave this assessment of the skills of Sunderland's workforce:

'The continued pre-eminence of Sunderland in shipbuilding affairs is what may be called the hereditary genius of its people for the industry. A shipbuilding port is not made in a day, or, indeed, in a single generation, and proximity to coal and iron fields counts for little as compared with the possession of a body of craftsmen who have inherited the cumulative skills, so to speak, of some hundreds of years of the trade. This indispensable equipment Sunderland happily enjoys …'

Left: The JL Thompson-built *Roma* on sea trials. The ship was launched from North Sands on 30th July 1901. It was the tenth vessel Thompson's had built for its owners Marwood's Steamship Company of Whitby.

A view of JL Thompson's showing how close the neighbouring streets were to the yard between the wars.

The launch of the *Bretwalda* from JL Thompson's on 18th August 1958 signalled the end of an era for shipbuilding on the Wear. The launch was the last from the 110 year old John Crown yard. JL Thompson's had bought the adjoining Crown's yard in 1946 and for the next dozen years it had retained its separate identity until Thompson's implemented a multi-million pound re-organization plan. This led to the dismantling of the single berth slipway and repair slipway to be replaced by a massive berth to accommodate the construction of 100,000 ton tankers.

The *Bretwalda* at sea (*right*) and plans for the vessel (*below*). The general cargo carrier was built for Hall Brothers Steamship Company.

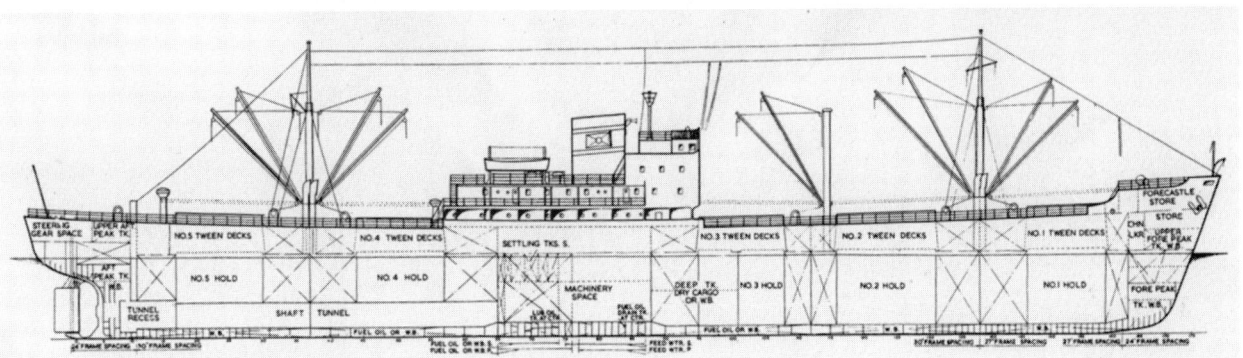

41

Two photographs taken by Brian Holden at JL Thompson's. Brian served his apprenticeship as a plater at the yard between 1958-64.

Two more photographs from Brian Holden's archives of JL Thompson's.

A 70,000 ton ship on the North Sands slipway. At this time in the 1970s the yard was capable of building ships of over 150,000 tons.

Above: A 70,000 ton Panamax class ship being built at JL Thompson's North Sands yard. At this time the yard was under the banner of the Sunderland Shipbuilders Group. Panamax ships were the largest that could navigate the Panama Canal.

Left: A multi-head profile-cutting machine at Sunderland Shipbuilders North Sands yard.

Men alongside the berth at JL Thompson's are dwarfed by the massive ship under construction.

The age of pre-fabrication in the assembly hall at North Sands in the 1970s.

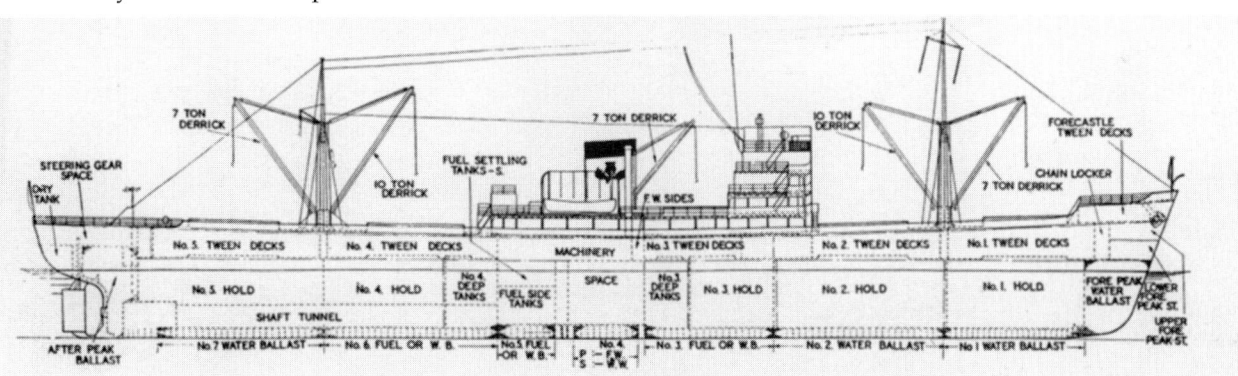

Plans for the 10,000 ton cargo ship *Thistledowne* built by JL Thompson's for the Albyn Line in 1952.

The JL Thompson's-built *Eastern Ranger* tied up alongside a 50,000 tanker under construction at North Sands. The *Eastern Ranger* was launched on 20th November 1961 for the Indo-China Steam Navigation Company. The day after the launch the *Eastern Ranger's* sister ship the *Eastern Rover* left the Wear on trials. She had been fitted out at Jl Thompson's in only ten weeks which a director of the owners described as a 'staggering achievement'.

Manor Quay

Above: The *Charlton Venus* fitting-out at JL Thompson's Manor Quay. The 16,500 ton motor tanker was launched from Doxford's on 19th June 1951 and at that time was the largest ship built at the Pallion yard.

Left: The 19,000 ton *British Willow* at Manor Quay in 1964 for fitting-out. The vessel is under the 150 ton hammer head crane which at that time was the largest on the Wear.

An aerial view of the Manor Quay before the Second World War.

Men working on a ship conversion at the Manor Quay.

Austin's

SP Austin & Son was founded in 1826 by Peter Austin who started building wooden collier brigs on the north side of the River Wear. Later his son joined the company and in 1846 they moved over the river to a site near Wearmouth Bridge which they occupied until they closed. A new drawing office and dock offices were built in the late 1890s when the company bought a site to the west of the yard that had formerly been a bottle works. An engine shop was also built and equipped at that time.

The yard suffered greatly during the hard times of the 1920s and '30s when Austin's made a loss every year from 1923 to 1936 – the only exception being 1929. In those years the total loss was £118,364. In 1936 it made a profit of only £415. The following year profits were up to £17,300. During the Second World War Austin's concentrated on replacing vessels in the coastal fleet that had been lost to German submarines and mines. A total of thirty-two vessels were built during the war as well as a frigate, the *Amberley Castle,* and also some landing craft. For a small yard such as Austin's this was an excellent contribution to the war effort. Austin's merged with Pickersgill's in 1954 and the yard closed ten years later. The demise of Austin's was partly brought about by the decline in the coal trade which had been a vital part of the company's business for many years.

Left: An advert for SP Austin and Son from the late 1940s.

A close up view of Austin's shipbuilding and repair yard. A ship is on the firm's pontoon which had been built by Swan Hunter's at Wallsend and was first used in 1903. The first ship to dock there was the Cunard Line SS *Brescia*. The pontoon, or floating dock, was able to accommodate ships up to 400 feet in length.

The *Nonsuch* on Austin's Pontoon. Austin's was famous for building ships for the coal trade and a busy time for the repair yard were the summer months when many colliers returned to the Wear for an overhaul. This was a time when there was a lull in exports as the winter months was the busiest time for colliers transporting coal.

Another view of the pontoon with Austin's shipyard berths in the distance.

Pickersgill's

William Pickersgill's built ships in the North Dock in the 1830s and '40s before moving to Southwick. William was killed in the yard in 1880 and his son, also called William, took over the firm and he stayed until the Second World War.

Above: The 9,200 ton *Hylton* was built as shipbuilding was emerging from the Depression. Launched from Pickersgill's on 31st October 1936 it was one of 36 vessels built on the Wear that year compared with only eight in 1935. It was the product of the government's Scrap and Build policy to bring work to shipyards. At 445 feet the *Hylton* was the longest vessel built at the yard up to that time.

Right: An advertisement from Wm Pickersgill's & Sons from around 1950.

Below: An aerial view of Pickersgill's in the 1930s.

Austin & Pickersgill's

In the 1950s Pickersgill's invested £3 million pounds to redevelop the yard. The reconstruction took four years with large assembly shops built and prefabrication introduced. Pickersgill's could now build ships up to 40,000 tons compared with 10,000 before redevelopment. In 1954 Austin's and Pickersgill's merged and ten years later shipbuilding was concentrated at Southwick.

In the mid 1970s there was further expansion at Austin & Pickersgill's and state of the art facilities were constructed that should have guaranteed a bright future for shipbuilding at Southwick. However, by the late 1980s the yard was closed and demolished a few years later.

A ship on the berth at Austin & Pickersgill's before redevelopment at the yard in the 1970s.

In the summer of 1976 Austin & Pickersgill's were featured on the cover of *100 A1* – the magazine of Lloyd's Register of Shipping. The cover picture showed Lloyd's Register ship surveyor Brian Costar looking on as a welder worked on a B26 bulk carrier. The magazine described Austin & Pickersgill's as one of 'Britain's most profitable shipbuilding companies'.

An Austin & Pickersgill's safety campaign poster from 1978.

Two contrasting views of launches from Austin & Pickersgill's. *Left*: Men look on as a ship enters the water from Pickersgill's in the 1950s. *Above*: Hard hats replace flat caps at a launch from Austin & Pickersgill's in the 1980s. This ship was built in the covered yard that provided working conditions that men in the '50s could only dream of.

Guests at the naming ceremony of the *Murree* at Austin & Pickersgill on 5th December 1980. High winds prevented the ship from being launched for thirteen days. The *Murree* was built for the Pakistan National Shipping Corporation.

Designers in Austin & Pickersgill's offices in the 1970s.

Foreman driller Alexander George Simpson retired from Austin & Pickersgill's on the last day of 1959 at the age of seventy. He had worked for the firm for 37 years and in total almost 55 years in local yards. He had started work in 1904 at Sir John Priestman's yard. During a shipbuilding slump he found work on the construction of Queen Alexandra Bridge. In 1922 he joined Pickersgill's where he remained until his retirement. Right up to the end of his working life Mr Simpson maintained that 'riveted ships are still better than welded ones.'

Above: The overhead magnetic crane in Austin & Pickersgill's plate stockyard in the 1970s.

Left: An aerial view of Austin & Pickersgill's showing the covered yard after modernization.

The 9,000 ton *Derwent* leaving Austin & Pickersgill's covered yard on 28th February 1979. The ship was launched by Mrs Dorothy Gawne, wife of the chairman of the owners, Royal Mail Line. Mrs Gawne said: 'I was terribly nervous but all went well.' Up till then the only vessel she had launched had been a narrow boat.

The double bottom and hopper assembly line at Austin & Pickersgill's in the late 1970s.

Bartram's

George Bartram began his shipbuilding firm in 1837 in partnership with John Lister. They were based at Hylton and their first ship was the *Crown* for William Thompson, a baker from Monkwearmouth. The shipbuilders made a profit of £77 on this ship launched in 1838. Bartram's partnership with Lister was dissolved in the 1850s and Bartram continued with his son until 1871 when the firm moved to the South Dock. This location made Bartram's the only yard in the country to launch ships directly into the sea. Sand would blow into the yard and weather was often very different on the coast than inland – although, conditions up river could be equally as harsh. In 1864 a launch from Bartram's yard at Hylton was postponed for a week because the river had frozen over.

In 1968 the firm was taken over by Austin's & Pickersgill's and ten years later was closed with the workforce moving to Southwick.

Right: An advertisement for Bartram's from the 1900s showing at this time the firm were building steamers for the Eastern Trade.

Below: A map showing Bartram's location (centre of picture) in relation to the North Sea. To the left of the yard is the North Eastern Marine Engine Works.

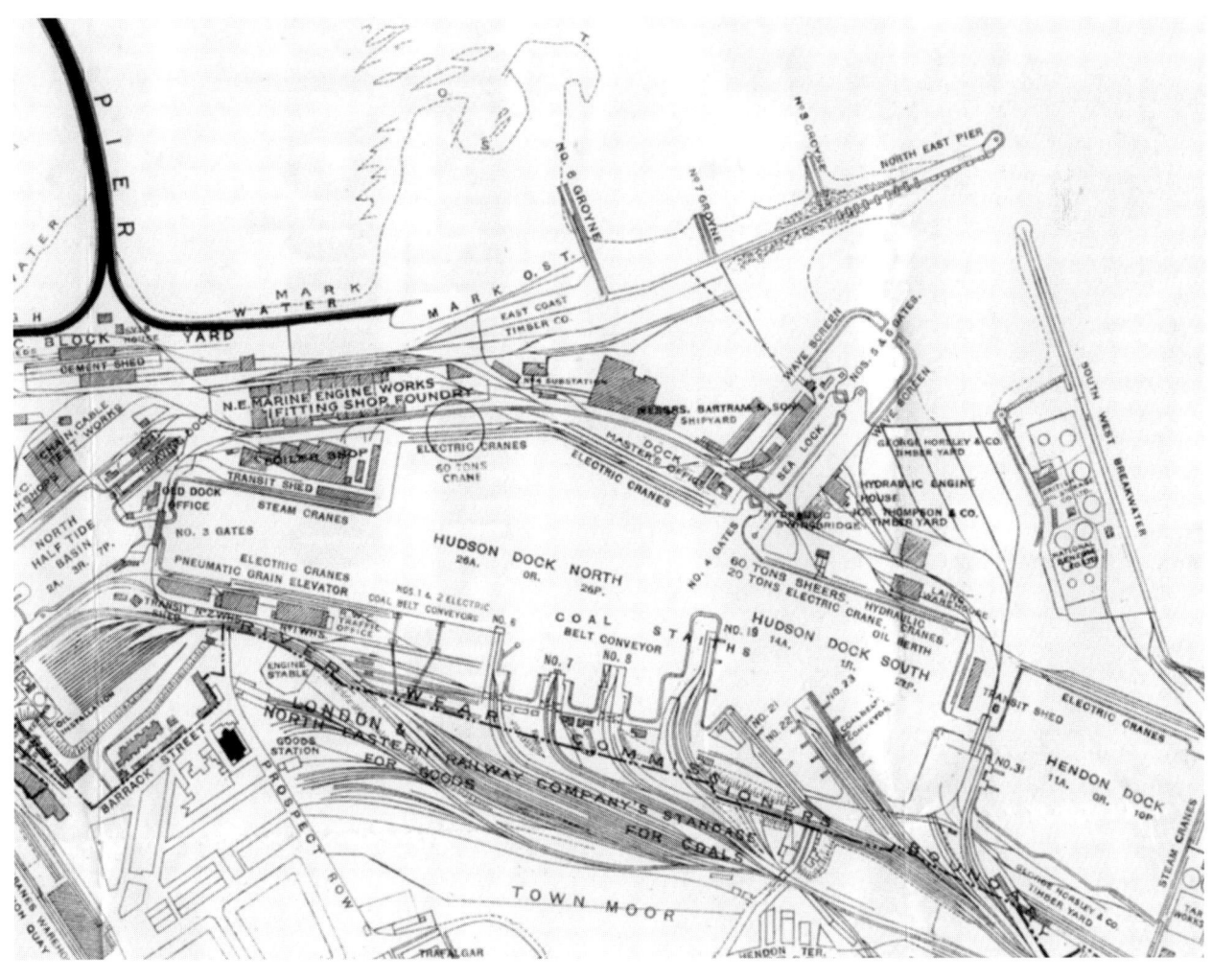

Above: The passenger-cargo liner TSMV *India* undergoing sea trials off Sunderland in 1950. Built for a Portuguese company, the ship was the largest passenger carrying vessel built in Sunderland at that time.

Right: Two interior photographs of TSMV *India* – the main staircase and the first class lounge and buffet. The vessel had been launched from Bartram's on 17th January 1950. Councillor C. McFetritch, one of the directors of Bartram's, said at the launch: 'It has been designed and built on the most luxurious scale and no expense has been spared by the owners to ensure that the *India* will be in the forefront of vessels of its class.'

When the *Jens Kofoed* was built at Bartram's she was described as the first car ferry to be built on the Wear. Her launch had to be postponed twice because of high winds before she finally went down the slipway on 9th May 1963. After being launched the *Jens Kofoed* was towed across the North Sea to be fitted-out in the Bremer Volkan yard in Germany. When the ferry went into service she carried 60 to 100 cars on the crossing between Copenhagen and the island of Bornholm.

James Cartwright's life in shipbuilding could not have started at a worse time. He joined JL Thompson's as a caulker in 1926 but the General Strike and the shipbuilding slump led to him joining the Army. During his seven year career in the Forces he trained as a welder at an Army Vocational Training Centre. He returned to Thompson's and later worked at Vickers-Armstrong. James joined Pickersgill's in 1938 and after the war joined Bartram's where he remained until he retired in 1975.

James Cartwright receiving a retirement gift from his workmates.

The MV *Australind* going down the slipway of Austin and Pickersgill's South Dock yard on 23rd March 1978. The launch of the SD14 had to be postponed a day because of high winds. However, Audrey Clarke, wife of chairman of the Australind Steam Shipping Company, performed the naming ceremony on the scheduled date. This was the last ever launch from the former Bartram's yard. Most of the men at the yard were transferred to Austin and Pickersgill's covered yard at Southwick. One of those who went up river was Jack Wilson who had worked at the South Dock for 45 years.

Laing's

One of Deptford's most famous sons was James Laing who was born in the shipyard of his father, Philip, in 1823. By the age of twenty, James took over the running of the family firm. Ten years later Laing's first iron-built ship, the *Amity*, was launched. In 1875 the magnificent *Torrens* was built and became one of the Wear's most remembered ships. She broke the sailing record to Adelaide in 64 days and the novelist Joseph Conrad was second mate from 1891 and 1893.

James Laing was knighted in 1897 and the yard changed its name to Sir James Laing & Sons. After his death the firm suffered severe losses and Sir James Marr took over. This other great shipbuilder steered Laing's back to financial security and the yard continued for a further 80 years. The last ship launched from Laing's was the *Mitla* on 3rd May 1985. The former shipyard is now the site of the crane manufacturer, Liebherr.

Right: An advert for Sir James Laing & Sons from the late 1920s. The aerial view shows how the yard was built on the bend of the river.

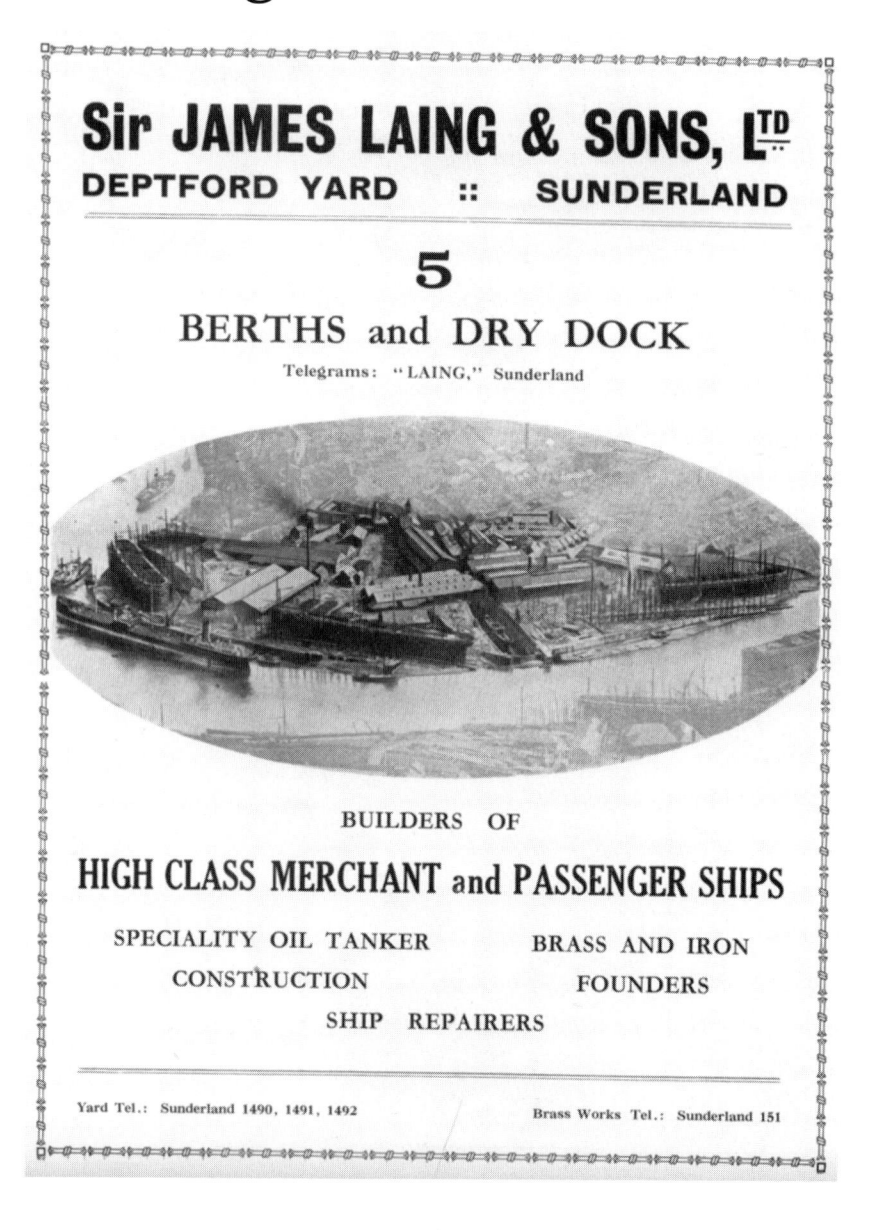

Sir JAMES LAING & SONS, LTD
DEPTFORD YARD :: SUNDERLAND

5 BERTHS and DRY DOCK

Telegrams: "LAING," Sunderland

BUILDERS OF
HIGH CLASS MERCHANT and PASSENGER SHIPS

SPECIALITY OIL TANKER CONSTRUCTION

BRASS AND IRON FOUNDERS

SHIP REPAIRERS

Yard Tel.: Sunderland 1490, 1491, 1492   Brass Works Tel.: Sunderland 151

Left: The Fleet repair ship HMS *Cyclops*. Conversion of the ship by Laing's in 1907 brought a heavy loss and put the firm in financial difficulties. James Marr was asked to join the firm to revive its flagging fortunes. He succeeded and Laing's became one of the leading yards on the river once again.

Two Wimpey jobs at Sunderland

New fitting-out berth

New launching berth

These new berths were constructed by Wimpeys for Sir James Laing & Sons' yard at Sunderland

WIMPEY

GEO. WIMPEY & CO. LTD., Regional Office, TEAMS STREET, DUNSTON, GATESHEAD-ON-TYNE (DUNSTON 84478)

An advert from Wimpey in the late 1940s which shows the redevelopment of Laing's shipyard. In 1946 W.B. Marr, chairman of Laing's, described Sunderland's great shipbuilding heritage: 'On a narrow river with many difficult bends and corners we manage to launch more merchant ship tonnage than any other town in the world.'

Right: A plater's Boilermakers' Society contribution card. In 1965 there were 567 platers working in Sunderland shipyards out of a total workforce of 7,059. Other trades at that time included: welders (1,077), shipwrights (568) and caulkers/burners (383). At this time there were only 25 riveters left on the Wear.

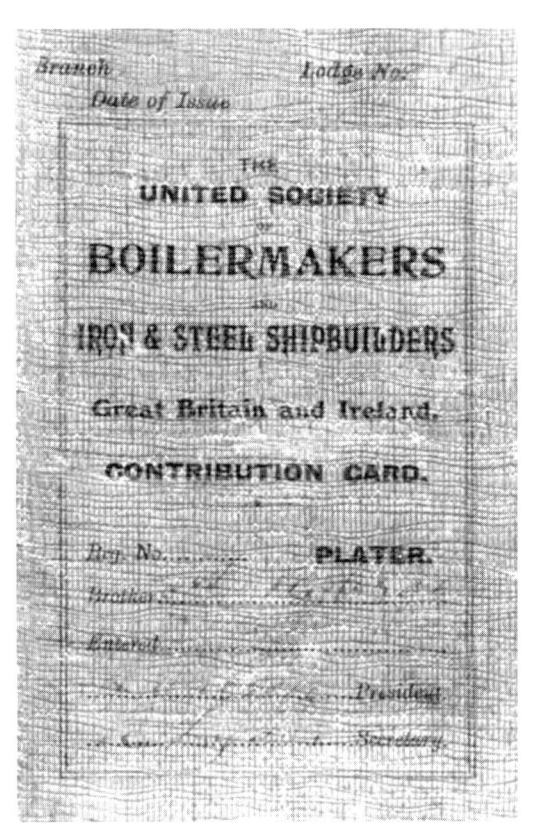

A gravity-feed welding machine at work in the assembly hall at Laing's in the 1970s.

A ship on the berths at Laing's in the mid 1980s. The final two ships built at the yard were the *Colima* (launched 30th July 1984) and the *Mitla* (launched on 3rd May 1985).

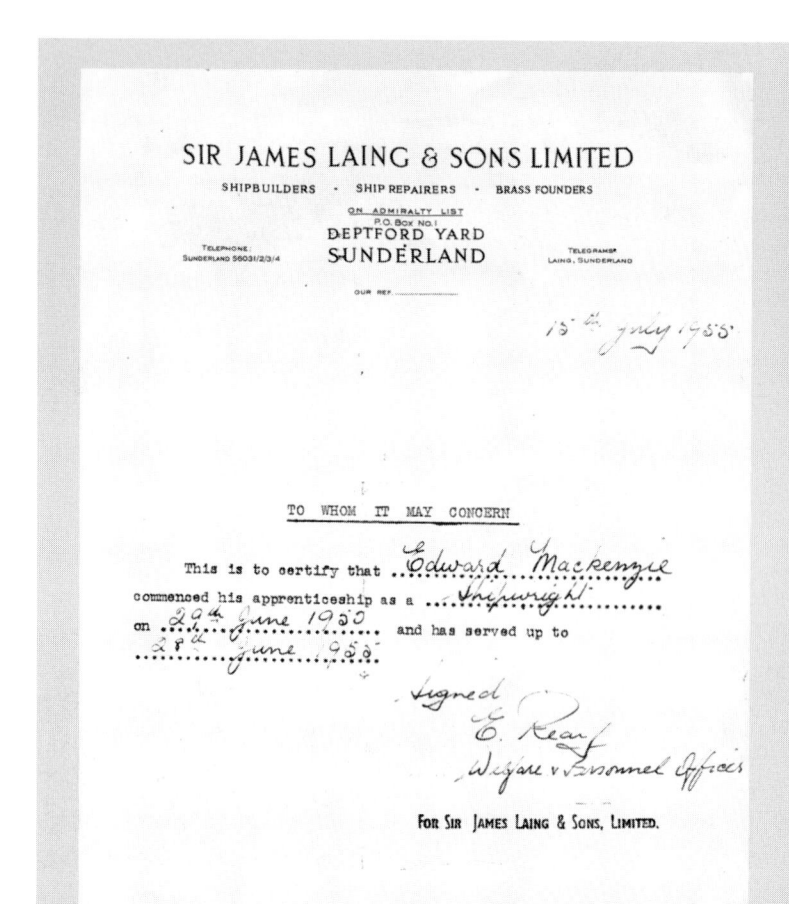

Edward 'Mac' Mackenzie (*above*) served his apprenticeship at Laing's in the 1950s. Mac was a shipwright and remembered his time in the yards with great affection. The trade of shipwright is an ancient one and there are references to a 'Company of Free Shipwrights' from 1387. Shipwrights even used an adze – a tool that dates back to biblical times.

Left: Mac's letter of certification from Laing's.

Two workers at Laing's take a break in 1970.

Short's

Short's was another shipbuilding firm who began at Hylton before moving down river. In 1870 they started building ships at Pallion near the old hall. Short's was very much a family yard. After the company was founded by George Short in 1850, his sons, grandsons (all nine of them) and great-grandsons worked at the yard. The firm survived for almost a century at Pallion before closing in 1964 with the loss of 300 jobs.

Right: George Short, the founder of the famous shipbuilding firm.

Above: Short's Mowbray Quay yard at Hylton in 1850.

Right: By the time this advertisement was produced in the 1900s Short Brothers was established as one of the main shipbuilders on the Wear. The ad proclaimed the firm built cargo, cattle and passenger steamers up to 700 feet in length.

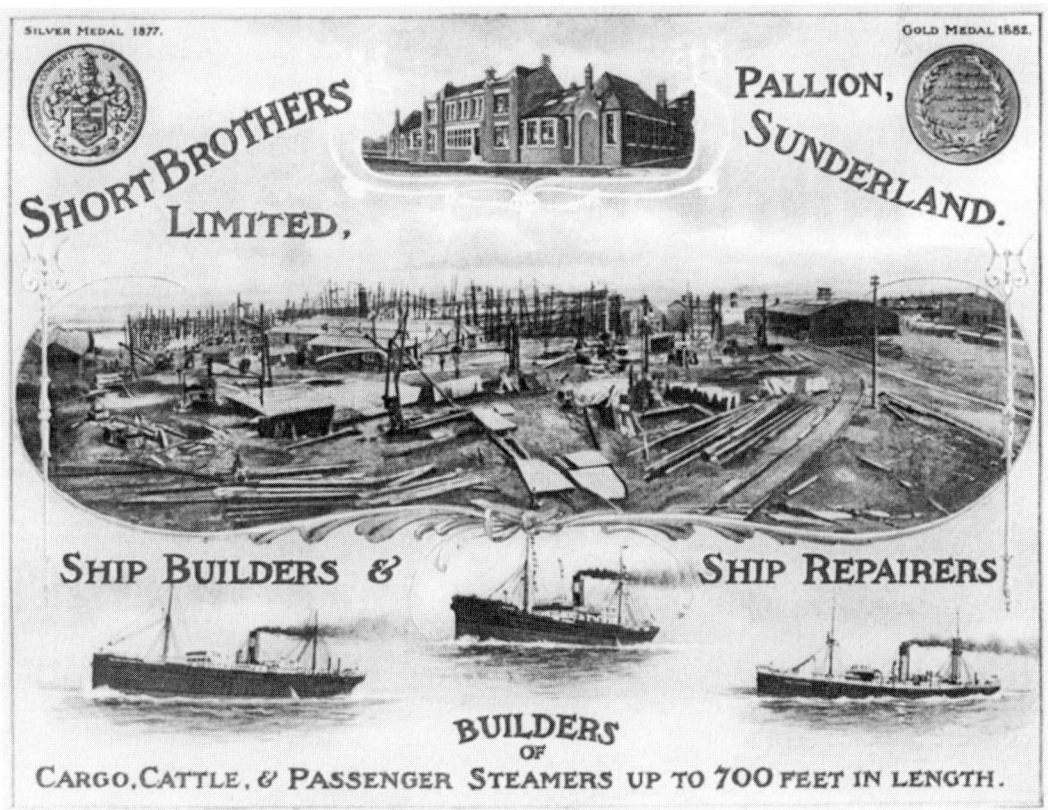

Builders of Cargo and Oil Tank Steamers
UP TO 13,000 TONS D.W.

SHORT BROTHERS, Ltd.,   Teleg.: "Short, Sunderland."   **SHIPBUILDERS**

PALLION SHIPYARD, **Sunderland**   Tel. No.: 2440 (3 lines).   **AND REPAIRERS**

An advert for the company from 1929.

Left: The 10,350 ton tanker *Soya Christina* was launched from Short's on 21st November 1949. The ship was built for Rederi A/B Soya of Stockholm.

The Last Ship

The 20,500 ton bulk carrier *Carlton* was the last ship built at Short's yard. The launch on 17th October 1963 from the old Pallion yard was delayed for over an hour. High winds had slowed preparations and when the *Carlton* started to move down the slipway it could only make inch by inch progress. It eventually gathered enough momentum to enter the water. The *Carlton* was the 19th ship built at the yard in 40 years for the Chapman and Willan Line of Newcastle.

A Deadly Legacy

Sunderland's boast of being the biggest shipbuilding town in the world came at a cost – the health of the workers. As one former shop steward said: 'We just got the conditions right in the yards, then they closed them down.' It was only in the final decades of shipbuilding on the Wear that health and safety was given the respect it deserved. For many years the working conditions of the men in the yards was considered secondary to making a profit.

Working in any heavy industry is a dangerous occupation but shipbuilding had its unique hazards:

Welder's Lung – Welding fumes filled the enclosed spaces men had to work in and there was sometimes very little ventilation. For many years the best ventilation welders had was provided by a 'windy pipe' extractor (using compressed air) but this could not take away all of the fumes. Some working areas were thick with fumes all day. It was not until the 1970s that men worked in an environment with safe ventilation. Now many suffer from the shortage of breath known as welder's lung.

Arthritis – Caused by the cold and often wet conditions. It could be cold even in the summer when working with steel plate and these conditions worsened in the winter. It was not until the 1970s that yards at Doxford's and Pickersgill's were covered and men were protected from the worst of the weather.

Arc Eye – The burning of a layer of skin in the eye caused by the welding rays. Many former welders and burners suffer from eye strain or poor eyesight.

Vibration White Finger – The pneumatic tools of the yards caused loss of feeling in the fingers.

Deafness – From the start of the shift to the end, men had to endure the noise of caulkers, riveters and drillers. By the 1970s the problems of shipyard noise was recognised and workers were encouraged to wear ear muffs.

Accidents – Falling equipment or materials – from nuts and bolts to rudders – caused numerous accidents. Men having to work at dangerous heights on narrow wooden battens also led to falls that were often fatal.

Some of these industrial diseases and illnesses could have been easily prevented. However, even simple protective clothing was not in common use until the later years of the yards. This included hard hats, ear muffs, safety glasses, welding capes and sleeves.

Welders in the assembly hall at the former Laing's yard at Deptford in the 1970s. By this time conditions in the yards had improved greatly but they were still dangerous places to work.

Asbestos

The dangers of the so called 'wonder material' asbestos were known from the 1930s but that did not stop its everyday use. It was not only common in the shipyards but could be found in factories, schools, offices and homes. There was even a major asbestos manufacturer at Washington – Newalls.

In the yards men worked directly with asbestos and breathed in its deadly fibres. It was widely used for the insulation of pipes in ship's engine rooms. Many men recall that by the end of their shift they would be covered in asbestos looking like 'snowmen or millers'. The wives of workers were also exposed to asbestos through fibres on their husband's work clothes. Sadly, some of the victims of this dangerous substance did not even work with it.

Campaigners who spent years trying to stop the use of asbestos came up against strong opposition from many in the industry. Eventually, its hazards were officially recognised and stricter controls were implemented in the early 1980s. However, this came too late for the many men and women who were exposed to its effects.

In Sunderland today diseases such as asbestosis, pleural plaques and mesothelioma among former workers is a sad legacy of their exposure to this deadly material.

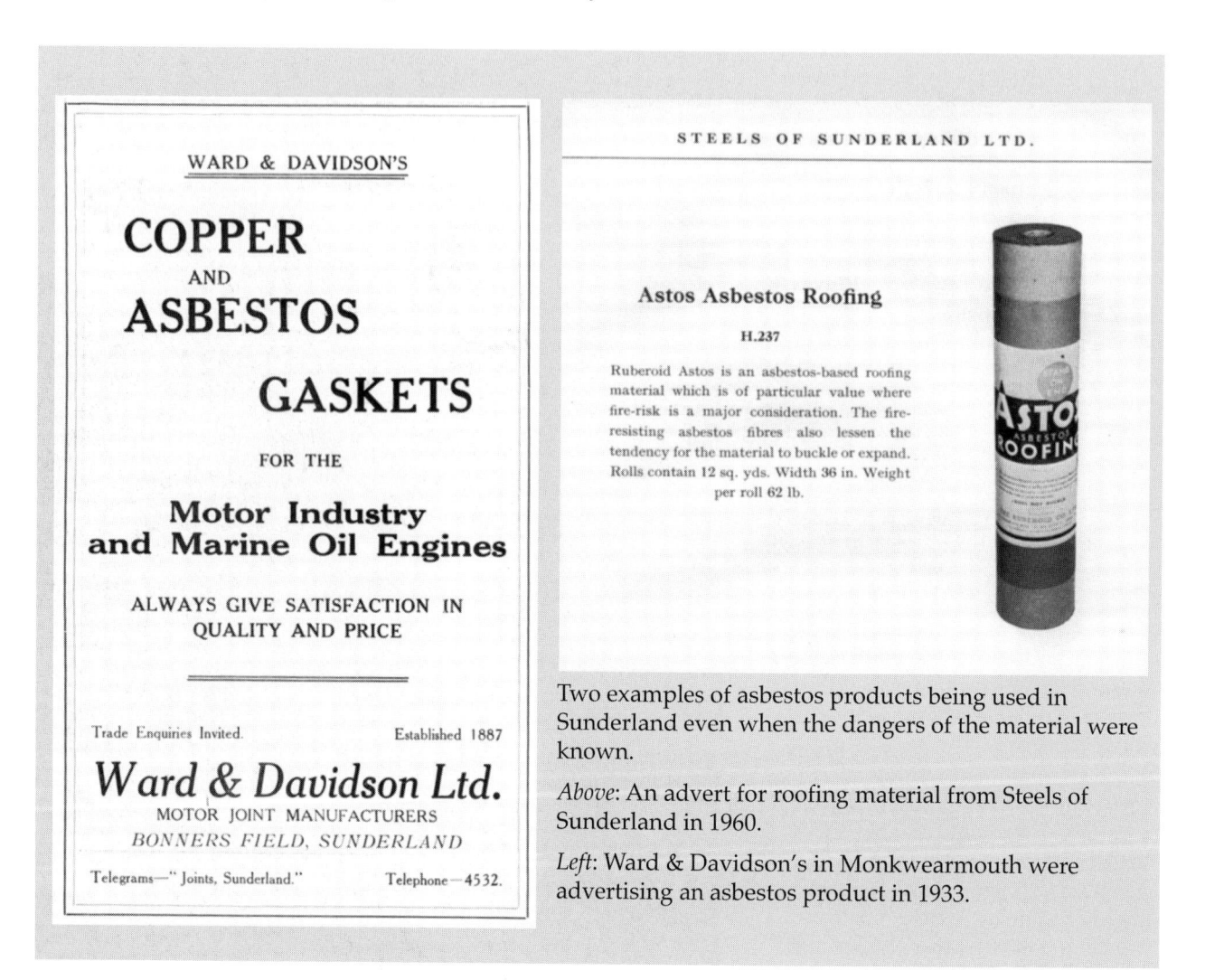

Two examples of asbestos products being used in Sunderland even when the dangers of the material were known.

Above: An advert for roofing material from Steels of Sunderland in 1960.

Left: Ward & Davidson's in Monkwearmouth were advertising an asbestos product in 1933.

Chapter Three

Building Ships For The World

The barque *Vencedora*, built by JL Thompson's for William Nicholson and Sons, Sunderland. This was the first ship launched at the firm's North Sands site. In 1946 a centenary brochure was produced by the company and it gave an early view of life at North Sands:

'On 13th February 1846 Robert Thompson & Sons established themselves on the site which was to become known throughout the world as a shipyard of renown. Robert Thompson took into partnership his sons Robert, Joseph Lowes and John. No agreement was made when he took possession of North Sands, the undertaking being that all partners would own equal shares. Robert Thompson Senior was to receive 30/- per week, Robert Thompson Junior 27/- per week and the other two some 24/- per week. The firm numbered eight all told at this early stage but that they could work was evident because they built a brig of 12 keels in eleven weeks. It should be remembered, of course, that work commenced at four in the morning and continued as long as daylight lasted.

'The first vessel built by this firm at North Sands was the brig *Pearl*, a favourable contract, on which they made £300. From this time forward the firm was continuously busy and their reputation for good shipbuilding began to be established. The launch of the first ship *Vencedora* was the occasion of great rejoicing. The apprentices followed the ancient custom and went through the ceremony of ducking and plunging into the water as soon as the ship was safely launched. Carpenters' allowances at this time were a pint of beer in the forenoon and afternoon for caulking, a pint of beer for the keel seam, and three pints of beer on the launching day.'

The launch of the *La Hogue* which at that time was the largest ship ever built in Sunderland. This picture is taken from *The Illustrated London News*, 11th August 1855. At 1,331 tons it was also the largest ship to be launched in the North of England at that time. It had been built by James Laing for Duncan Dunbar and was used in the Australian trade. At that time emigrants were transported from Britain to Australia while wool would be carried on the return journey.

Three Launches in an Hour

Even by Sunderland standards when three launches a day was not uncommon, the 6th March 1947 was a red letter day for shipbuilding on the Wear. On this day three ships went down the slipways within sixty minutes of each other along a 200 yard stretch of the Wear above Queen Alexandra Bridge. The first to enter the water was the 9,800 ton *Hartismere* from Doxford's. Fifteen minutes later the 9,100 ton steamer *Aida* went down the slipway from Short Brothers' Pallion yard. The final launch from Pickersgill's did not go as smoothly as the first two. The 10,000 ton *Lord Glanely* crashed into Short's fitting-out quay on the opposite bank of the river damaging its rudder and propeller. Forty workmen watching the launch from the quay had to run for safety as the huge stern of the *Lord Glanely* headed towards them. Shipwright George Curtis said he expected to see the *Lord Glanely* pull up in midstream but the vessel continued to come towards them scattering men on the quay. Another shipwright, James Nash, recalled how he rushed into the painters' shop to warn the men to run for safety but fortunately no one was inside.

Above: The SS *Aida* one of the three ships launched in an hour. A centenary brochure produced by Short's in 1950 gives this account of the unusual story of the *Aida*:

'An interesting feature in connection with the SS *Aida*, built for a company based in Stockholm, in 1947, was the flying from Sweden of the crew, direct to Sunderland, by a Catalina flying boat. Special permission had to be obtained from the London Headquarters of HM Customs before the flying boat was allowed to come into the Wear with the twenty-four men for the vessel. The flying boat touched down outside the main pier and taxied up to the lower buoys before discharging its passengers.'

The Swedish crew of the *Aida* arrive in Sunderland on board a Catalina flying boat.

The torpedo boat *El Rayo* built at Doxford's in the 1880s. Here it is on slips for 'cleaning up' in 1887. An article from *The Syren and Shipping* in 1929 gave a colourful account of the history of this vessel:

'In 1886 the firm built on their own account a typical single-screw torpedo boat, which they named the *El Rayo*. She was originally fitted with a coal-burning locomotive boiler, and on her trials attained a speed of 21 knots, the highest hitherto recorded for that type of craft. She was shortly afterwards converted for oil-burning – at that time quite an innovation – and ran several very successful trials on the new fuel, including a full-speed trial without a trace of smoke, which is more than can be said of some of the present day oil burners. She was, however, before her time and was not taken over by the British Government. For some time she lay on the builders' hands, but was ultimately bought by 'private owners'. Individuals, it may be remarked, do not go to war on their own account, and the fact that the vessel was afterwards heard of in Venezuela at the time of the Revolution leads one to suppose that the buyers had their clients in view at the time of the purchase.'

Sunderland Shipbuilders and Shiprepairers

The *Port of Sunderland Guide* for 1948 listed the shipbuilders and shiprepairers who were at work in Sunderland at that time:

Name of Firm	Number of Berths	Length of Berths (Feet)	Length of Fitting-out Quay (Feet)
SP Austin & Son	3	310 / 325 / 268	250
Bartram & Sons	3	450 each	500
John Crown & Sons	2	335 each	
William Doxford & Sons	6	Up to 550	600
Sir James Laing & Sons	5	Up to 590	330
William Pickersgill & Sons	5	Up to 450	–
The Shipbuilding Corporation (Wear Branch)	3	440 each	–
Short Brothers	4	3 – 430 / 1 – 350	544
Joseph L Thompson & Sons	4	470 / 475 / 445 / 430	700
TW Greenwell & Company		Ship and Engine Repairs only	

Tale of Two Princesses

The launch of the MV *British Princess* from Laing's on 30th April 1946. The ship had been named by a princess – Princess Elizabeth who six years later would become our Queen. Thousands of spectators crowded the banks of the Wear to witness the launch and at Laing's there were 6,000 ticket holders allowed inside – 4,000 of these were workers and their wives. Men at the Deptford yard used every vantage point to get a glimpse of the launch with some climbing on to cranes and machinery while others stood on the *Empire Naisby* which was being fitted-out at the nearby quay. Flat caps were thrown into the air as the ship went down the slipway and there was a scramble to collect broken pieces of the shattered bottle used to name the vessel.

The *British Princess* was to have a working life of less than fifteen years. In July 1961 she was one of six ships sold by BP Tanker Company for scrap. The *British Princess* had been laid up in Swansea for more than two years before finally being scrapped by the British Iron and Steel Corporation.

Princess Elizabeth makes her way through Laing's shipyard on the way to the launch. Sir William Fraser, chairman of the Anglo-Iranian Oil Company, holds his umbrella over the Princess to shelter her from the pouring rain. Surtees Gleghorn, on the left, doffs his cap as she passes by. There was cheering as the Princess walked though Laing's and she waved to the workers and their families who were packed into the yard. After the launch the future Queen was presented with a flower brooch in a silver box. It was engraved 'British Princess.' The Princess had her lunch prepared and served by the canteen staff at the yard.

The Biggest Shipbuilding Town In The World

The authors of the *Where Ships Are Born*, the excellent history of Sunderland shipbuilding published after the Second World War, gave a detailed account of why Sunderland claimed the title the biggest shipbuilding town in the world.

In 1819, in the days of wooden ships, it was said: 'The Wear shipbuilding business in the port stands the highest of any in the United Kingdom, and gives employment to a great number of carpenters.' In 1834 Lloyd's Register said that Sunderland's output almost equalled the gross tonnage of all the other shipbuilding towns put together.

In later years rivers such as the Clyde and the Tyne would build more ships than Sunderland but in Scotland and Tyneside their shipbuilding industries were spread over several communities. On the Clyde their were yards in Glasgow and Greenock while on the Tyne ships were built in Wallsend, Jarrow and South Shields. It was only on the Wear that the industry was centred in one community and so Sunderland claimed the title of the biggest shipbuilding town in the country. Sunderland also had no equal throughout the world. In some years the town's output almost matched that of the whole of the United States of America.

The launch of the *Høegh Arrow* from Laing's on 19th July 1950. The ship, a 23,000 ton tanker, was at that time the largest ship ever built on the Wear. The previous record was held by the 16,000 ton *British Reliance*, built by Laing's the previous year. There were 5,000 people inside the yard to witness the launch from the biggest berth on the river – with thousands more crowding the banks of the Wear. The police had to ask some spectators to leave their vantage point at the Low Quay on the opposite bank as there were fears of a large wash when the ship entered the water. However, there were to be no problems with the launch with extra drag chains used to control the ship.

The Half Crown Ship

When the aft end of the *Rondefjell* was launched from the Strand slipway of John Crown's yard on 9th April 1951 it was hailed as the first tanker in the world to be built in two parts. Crown's yard was too small to build the complete 565ft vessel so the 290ft bow section followed six months after the first section. The two halves of the *Rondefjell* were joined together in dry dock at South Shields.

The 9,800 ton MV *Port Saint John* entering the river from JL Thompson's on 9th August 1937. The ship was launched only 11 weeks after the first frame was erected. The yard was disappointed that the deckhouse was not built before the launch. This was due to delays in steel deliveries because of shortages in raw materials.
(Courtesy of Sunderland Museum and Winter Gardens – Tyne and Wear Museums)

HM Coastal Minesweeper *Kedleston* on the Wear after it was launched from Pickersgill's on 23rd December 1953. The vessel was the first built for the Admiralty on the Wear since the Second World War. As this was the launch of a Naval ship there was a more elaborate ceremony than usual. The Rev T.A. Bendelow, Rector of Holy Trinity Church, Southwick, conducted a service from the launch platform. The service was broadcast throughout the yard using loudspeakers. When the ship was launched there was a chorus of *Hearts of Oak* and then the National Anthem was played when the ship was in the water.

The launch of the *Baron Ardrossan* at Pickersgill's on 5th April 1954. The 9,000 ton steamer was built for the Glasgow company, H. Hogarth & Sons, who named all of their ships after Scottish Barons. *Baron Ardrossan* was their 62nd ship in 73 years of trading and the fifth to use this title – one of the titles of the Earl of Eglinton.

A view of JL Thompson's looking from the sea. As the North Sands complex expanded over the years it took over the yards of Pile, Austin, Blumer and Crown.

Two Tugs From Thompson's

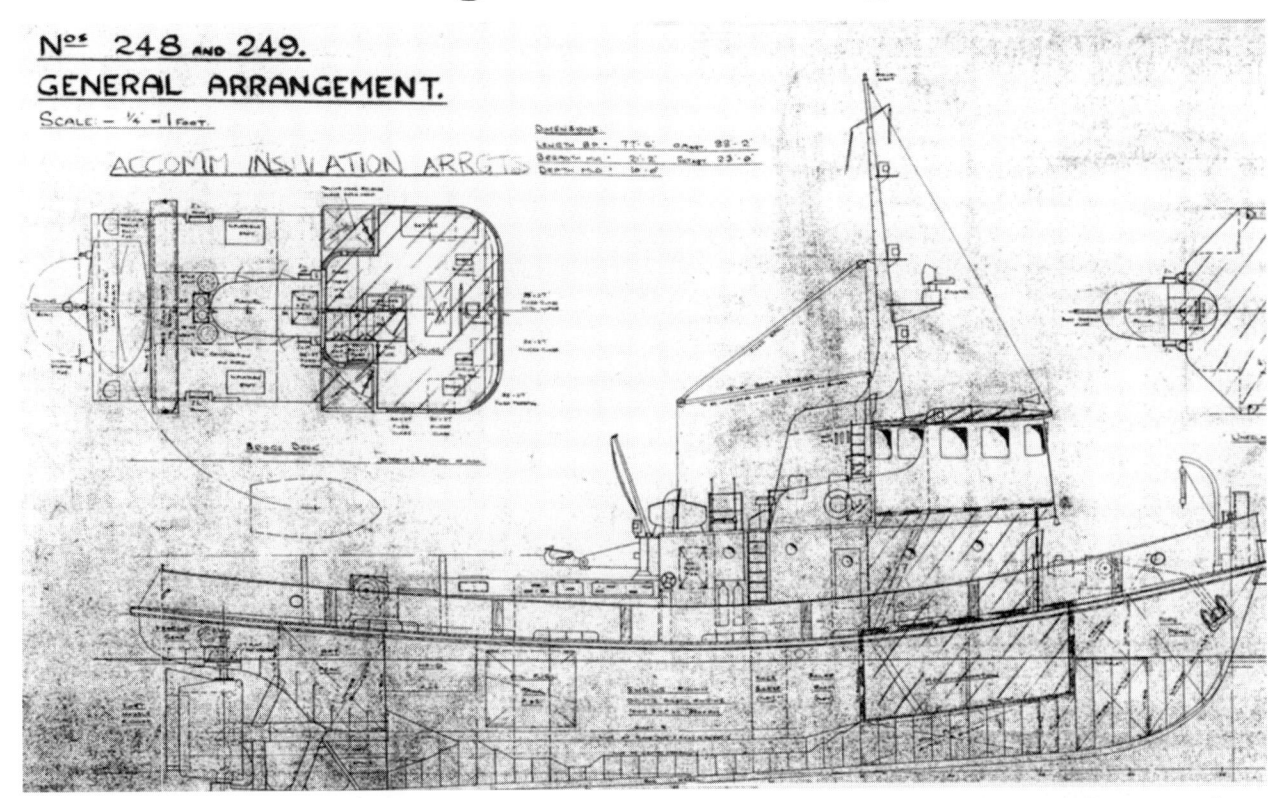

The plans for two identical tugs built for JL Thompson's for the Clyde Shipping Company of Glasgow. The *Flying Witch* and *Flying Wizard* were launched within minutes of each other on 9th June 1960. A special launch platform was built alongside the vessels. They were the first tugs to be built on the Wear after the Second World War.

The *Flying Witch* during trials before being handed over to her owners. The single screw motor tug recorded a speed of $11^3/_4$ knots and a static pull of $13^1/_2$ tons.

The Decline of the Steamer

The years after the Second World War saw the rapid decline of steamers built on the Wear in favour of motor ships. At the end of 1949 there were 10 steamers on the stocks or being fitted-out in Sunderland yards. By the end of the following year there were only five.

The Laing's-built *Sherburn* at the port of Dieppe in the early 1900s. The iron screw steamer was launched from the Deptford yard on 28th July 1866. The *Sherburn* was built for Lambton Collieries for work in the coal trade.

Two views of the *Atomena* at sea. The 14,000 ton vessel was launched from Laing's on 16th May 1961. The *Atomena* was one of three vessels Laing's built that year. The others were the *Mogen* and *Teakwood*.

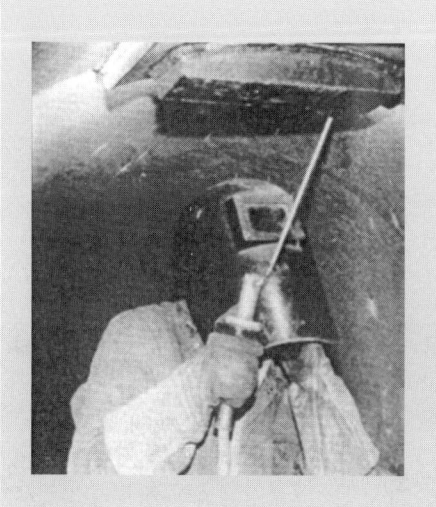

The Lads Knew Best

Speaking after a launch in December 1948 R. Cyril Thompson said: 'Unless more young men decide to become riveters the time is coming when shipowners will have no option but to take welded vessels. It is well known that on this river the number of riveters is diminishing very quickly. We cannot get apprentices to become riveters because they think it is a dying trade and consequently they will not serve their time in it.'

Despite the plea from shipbuilders like Thompson, young lads in Sunderland realised that their future lay in welding (*left*) and not riveting

Canon Hopkins, in his book *Pallion: Church and People in a Shipyard Parish*, gave this account of a launch on the Wear:

'At a launch you do not see great signs of enthusiasm on the part of the workers who have built the ship, and who watch her take the water – but if you listen to the casual comments which pass from one man to another, you know very well that it means a good deal to a man to see the fruits of his labour gracefully take the water. Again, when she is due to leave the quay and go down the river and out to sea on her trials, you know that a great many eyes are on her, and the men in the yard who built her are commenting on her lines, and her finish, and the joiners will have a good deal to say about her furnishings and fittings. Then, as she goes down the river towards the mouth, past the various other shipyards which are to be found both sides of the river, the fellows who are at work in those yards will knock off for a minute while she passes and they will carefully weigh her up and eye her just as critically as a racing man will look over the points of a horse, and make their judgements accordingly.'

The iron sailing barque *General Picton* under sail. The ship was built at Austin and Son's Wear Dock Yard and launched on 26th May 1884. This was the second vessel built at the yard for owners Thomas Morris and partners of Aberystwyth.

The general cargo carrier *Baltic Venture*. The vessel was launched from Doxford's on 20th November 1964. It was constructed with an ice breaker bow and ice fin and knives at the stern to allow her to cut through the frozen Baltic Sea. Chairman and managing director, Clem Stephenson, described the *Baltic Venture* as one of the strongest ships Doxford's had ever built.

Right: The 16,000 ton *Silksworth* launched from North Sands on 28th February 1964.

The 31,000 ton *Johanna Oldendorff* at the Manor Quay. The multi-purpose container carrier was launched from Austin & Pickersgill's on 3rd November 1986 and joined a sister ship *Dietrich Oldendorff* launched earlier in the year. In 1971 Austin & Pickersgill's had built the *Dorthe Oldendorff* followed in the next few years by the *Imme Oldendorff*, *Hille Oldendorff*, *Heinrich Oldendorff* and *Catherina Oldendorff*

Left: The 34,750 ton Laing's-built *Flisvos*. Eighteen-year-old Despina Fafalios, the daughter of John Fafalios, performed the naming ceremony at the launch of the *Flisvos* on 7th October 1971.

The Last Days of William Pile

The *Rodney* launched from William Pile's yard in March 1874. This was one of the last ships the yard built. Pile had died suddenly at the age of 50 and the *Rodney* and two other vessels were completed for the executors.

The *Rodney* was built for Devitt and Moore of London and the fully rigged iron ship was intended to sail between Melbourne and South Australia. In the 1890s the *Rodney* was sold to a French company and was renamed *Gipsy*. After a short period of service she was wrecked on the Scilly Isles in 1901.

A large crowd gathered on the banks of the Wear on 14th May 1874 for a special occasion – not only was it a double launch but it was the last from William Pile's yard. The 1,764 ton sailing ship *Plassey* and the 877 ton fully rigged *Olive* went into the water from Pile's yard.

After they were launched the *Plassey* was taken to the Bridge Dock and the *Olive* to the North Dock to be rigged-out. Meanwhile, the launch guests retired to the Draughting Loft to have luncheon where the success of the vessels was drunk with 'great enthusiasm'.

**WILLIAM PILE, JUN.,
SHIP BUILDER, REPAIRER, & SAW MILLS,
North Sands,
SUNDERLAND.**

An advert for the famous Monkwearmouth shipbuilder from 1860.

The *Plassey* was built for the East India trade and the *Olive* for the China and India trade. The *Sunderland Times* declared the Plassey was 'undoubtedly the finest specimen of marine architecture ever produced on the Wear.'

The authors of *Where Ships Are Born* were in no doubt of the importance of William Pile in Sunderland's shipbuilding history:

'Pile lived to see the peak of perfection in sailing ship design. He had contributed in a great measure towards the establishment of Sunderland as the largest shipbuilding town in the world.'

The *Sheaf Mount* being towed to the fitting-out quay after being launched from JL Thompson's on 3rd November 1964.

A ship under construction at Laing's. Today, the Liebherr works occupy the site of the Deptford yard.

The 9,100 ton vessel *Rio Gualeguay* was built at Short's and launched on 27th August 1946 for the Argentine company, Flota Mercante del Estado. The ship had the latest accommodation facilities with special quarters for seven apprentices.

The *Rio Gualeguay*'s sister ship, *Rio Diamante* launched from Short's on 30th May 1946, was the first Argentine Merchant Navy vessel to be built in Britain. The ships were to be used to carry food from South America to Europe which had severe shortages in the post Second World War years. On the day of the launch of the *Rio Gualeguay*, Captain Teodora E. Hartung, Chief of the Argentine Naval Commission in London said: 'They will bring great relief to the needy people of the world by carrying large quantities of the finest foods to them. I pray to God we shall be granted record harvests so that we can share them gladly with all those so sorely in need.'

A third Argentine ship, the *Rio Tueco*, was launched on 11th November 1946. By that time the first vessel, *Rio Diamante*, had sailed the 6,000 miles to Buenos Aires and was ready to return to Europe with a cargo of grain.

The *Fayrouz IV* was launched by ten-year-old Jade El Mehdawi on 22nd September 1983 from Austin & Pickersgill's. On the same day he had performed the naming ceremony of the *Fayrouz III*. He was the grandson of the Greek owner Thomas Demseris of the Ferenki Shipping and Trading Company of Piraeus. Jade's sister, Fayrouz, had named the first two ships of the £40 million order which were also named after her.

The *Sprucebank* launched from Doxford's on 10th June 1964.

A Lifetime of Launches

The launch of the *Orient City* on 24th November 1976 was a special occasion for Norman Gothard – it was his 161st and final launch at Laing's. After serving his apprenticeship as a blacksmith with Laing's he was to remain with the firm for a total of fifty years.

Left: The 19,000 ton British Petroleum tanker *British Beech*. At the ship's launch from Laing's on 26th May 1964 Mr J. Houston Jackson, managing director of BP tanker Company, said the *British Beech* was the 179th vessel built for his company in the last 19 years. Laing's had built no less than 22 ships of this total.

The 85,600 ton tanker *Borgsten*. When the *Borgsten* was launched from JL Thompson's on 1st November 1963 she was the biggest tanker ever built in Britain and the largest merchant ship since the *Queen Elizabeth*. A large crowd gathered on the opposite bank of the river for the launch. When the ship went down the slipway, after a 13 minute delay, there was a great roar from the thousands gathered to see the giant vessel enter the water. The Norwegian owner praised JL Thompson's as they were the only British yard willing to take the risk to build such a great tanker.

Right: The *Borgsten*'s main switchboard supplied by Sunderland Forge. At the time this was the largest the company had designed and built.

Left: SS *Wychwood*, launched from Austin's on 12th September 1950. Two other ships were launched in Sunderland that day. The largest was the 8,800-ton *King City* built at Doxford's. It was to be the last ship built at the old West Yard. There was also a launch over the river at Pickersgill's when the collier *Sir Archibald Page* entered the water. All three ships were launched within a hour of each other.

Above: The 14,800 ton *Sinaia* was launched from Laing's on 9th March 1966 by the wife of the Romanian ambassador to Britain. This was one of an order of two ships for Romania worth £2³/₄ million.

All Ships Built

Bartram's built a number of different types of ships in their yard in the South Dock. An advert in 1960 described some of those they had sent down their slipway:

Turakina (fully refrigerated vessel) 8,200 ton dwt, launched 26th February 1960

India (cargo/passenger) 6,700 ton dwt, launched 17th January 1950

George Lyras (tanker) 16,700 dwt, launched 22nd April 1955

Wandby (bulk carrier) 15,800 dwt, launched 24th April 1959

Silverbeck (general cargo) 13,800 dwt, launched 4th September 1959

La Loma (carriage of motor cars) 14,500 ton dwt, launched 12th December 1958

By the end of the 1960s Bartram's concentrated on building SD 14s as part of the Austin & Pickersgill group.

The Bank Line

The Bank Line shipping company had a long association with Sunderland shipbuilders. Their first vessel built on the Wear was the *Gifford*, launched from Doxford's in 1913.

Right: Lady Inverforth, wife of the chairman of the Bank Line, at Doxford's for the naming of the *Cedarbank* on 9th April 1976. The vessel was the 46th ship built in Sunderland for the Bank Line Company part of the Andrew Weir Group. Also that day, Lady Inverforth started an engine on the test bed at the nearby Doxford Engine Works.

The day before, the new Pallion covered yard had been officially opened by Lord Melchett, Parliamentary Under Secretary to the Department of Industry.

On the 26th May the *Cedarbank* was the first ship to be floated out of the 'shipbuilding factory'.

Below: An advert for the Bank Line from 1979.

The *Riverbank* built at Doxford's in 1977. The vessel was the 50th ship built on the Wear for the Bank Line Company. To commemorate this achievement the shipping company paid for a 'worker's garden' to be laid out at the Pallion yard.

Right: The MV *Troutbank* undergoing sea trials. The vessel had been launched from Laing's shipyard in 1979. In the late 1970s a detailed report of the *Troutbank* was compiled by Captain W. Watson for the Bank Line magazine. Here Captain Watson describes the launch of the *Troutbank* from Laing's on 26th April 1979:

'Previous to the launch, activity around the slipway increased as the latter was prepared with a heavy waxy grease – melted in pots on open fires on the berth. All chocks and wedges were connected to wires and ropes for recovery and clearance, and bilge chocks were removed.

At Deptford shipyard, because the river width and launching basin is limited, several tons of anchor chain are attached to the ship's side with wire pennants. These act as drag chains to slow down the speed of the vessel as soon as she has left the slipway. Three pairs of chains were used at *Troutbank's* launch, a total of 300 tons.

On launch day, shipwrights start knocking out chocks and shores from under the ship commencing from aft, one squad to port and one squad to starboard. Both squads are careful to progress up the slipway together and end under the fore part of the ship at the same time. When the last shores and wedges are clear forward, the ship is then held only by the launch triggers and when these are released, the launch starts.

By the time the vessel enters the water, over a distance of 1,000 feet, from a standing start she has reached a speed of about 15 knots and has experienced the greatest acceleration she will ever reach in her life. From then on, the drag chains take over and slow the ship until tugs take her in tow and bring her back alongside.'

The *Troutbank* under construction at Laing's.

Above: The *Finnamore Meadow* during sea trials. She went down Austin & Pickersgill's slipway on 6th September 1961. From laying the keel to its launch it only took the yard 46 working days to complete the vessel. The 18,000 ton ore carrier had an overall length of just over 500ft. It could reach a speed of 12 knots when fully loaded.

Left: The wheelhouse of the *Finnamore Meadow*.

A Short Life

The SD 14 *Santa Artemis* was launched from Bartram's on 20th September 1971. On her maiden voyage she collided in fog with a ship off the coast of South Africa and sank.

The *Surrey Trader* was launched from Austin & Pickersgill's on 15th January 1964.

The launch of the MV *Port Quebec* from JL Thompson's on 17th August 1939. The 10,000 ton vessel had been built for the Port Line company in only three months (including a break when the yard closed for the holidays). The shipbuilder's chairman, Major R. Norman Thompson, said at the launch: 'We were most grateful for the confidence the Port Line placed in us when they gave us the order. At that time we had only one vessel on the stocks and the order kept the yard going – so you will readily understand what it meant to us.'

The 24,500 ton *Kollfinn* at JL Thompson's. The bulk carrier was launched from the North Sands yard on 25th March 1963 for Norwegian owners.

The tugs *Ryhope* and *Grangetown* on the Wear with a steam paddle tug behind. JL Thompson's yard can be seen in the background on the left with the Garths on the right. The last paddle tug on the river was the *Eppleton Hall*. She left Sunderland in 1964 to work at Seaham then five years later sailed across the Atlantic to become an exhibit in a San Francisco Bay maritime museum. Tugs played an essential role in shipbuilding on the Wear. Once vessels were launched they relied on tugs to manoeuvre them to the fitting-out quays.

The *Helvellyn* launched from Robert Thompson & Sons on 21st April 1856. This was one of four ships the yard built that year. The others were the *Cumberland*, *Eliza Sharp* and *Sea Venture*.

All The World Was Their Stage

Over the years Sunderland's reputation for building good quality ships at a fair price brought orders from every part of the globe. In the 1890s and 1900s JL Thompson's built a number of vessels for US companies. The North Atlantic Steamship Company and the New York & Pacific Steamship Company were two of the American owners who had ships supplied by Wear yards.

Europe was a traditional market for Sunderland yards. Before the First World War yards built ships for German owners but this soon ended when hostilities commenced.

As early as 1896 Short's launched the *Leonidas* for Greek owners. However, it was the post-war years that saw the boom in Greek shipping and yards on the Wear built over 100 vessels for owners like Nicholas G. Livanos, Rethymnis & Kulukundis and the Chandris Group.

Austin & Pickersgill's was fortunate to have Greek-born Basil Mavroleon heading the company and his contacts among his countrymen brought in many orders.

Ships were also constructed for Sweden, Norway, Denmark, Holland, France and, in later years, the *Sinaia* was one of two ships built for Romania.

On the 8th March 1966 the refrigerated cargo-liner *Tekeo* was launched from Bartram's. It was the second of three ships built for the New Zealand Shipping Company.

Other destinations for Sunderland ships included: Australia, Mexico, Argentina, Cuba, India, Pakistan, Ethiopia, Egypt, Japan, Hong Kong and China.

The *Nippon Maru* was built by Laing's for Toyo Kisen Kabushiki Kaisha of Tokyo. Sir James Laing launched the twin screw mail and passenger ship on 23rd April 1898. The engines of the *Nippon Maru* were built by George Clark of Sunderland. The ship had accommodation for 100 first class passengers.

The *Ravensworth* was launched from Austin & Pickersgill's on 6th October 1960. The ore carrier was built for Dalgliesh of Newcastle to go on charter for the British Iron & Steel Corporation.

Right: The *Exning* on sea trials. The general cargo vessel was launched from Austin & Pickersgill's on 29th November 1964.

Without Ceremony

When the *Tactician* was launched from Doxford's on 16th February 1961 it went into the water without ceremony. The *Tactician* was the 16th ship Doxford's had built for the Harrison Line of Liverpool and few of these had traditional naming ceremonies on launch day.

Price Rises

When the SD 14 was introduced in 1968 they cost £915,000 each but by 1982 the price of each vessel had soared to £6¼ million.

Left: The 46,000 ton bulk carrier *Mylla*. When launched on 14th November 1966 it was the largest ship ever built at Laing's Deptford yard up to that time.

The *Challenger* – the last vessel launched from JL Thompson's in November 1986. The massive crane ship had been built for ITM Offshore of Middlesbrough but before the vessel was completed the Teesside company went into receivership. The Sunderland yard still went ahead with the £45 million order and the *Challenger* was a familiar sight on the Wear until a new owner was found.

The *Stena Seawell* at the Manor Quay. She had been launched from Doxford's on 12th March 1986. This and her sister ship, the *Stena Wellserver*, were maintenance ships for the North Sea oil field.

Two views of the 11,000 ton *Geddington Court*. Ready for launch from Short's yard on 5th March 1954 (*left*) and heading down river (*above*).

Women in the Shipyards

During both world wars hundreds of women worked in Sunderland shipyards. *Where Ships Are Born* described Bartram's yard as having the first woman welder to be admitted to the Boilermakers' Society. Mrs Collard started in July 1942 and worked at the yard throughout the war.

Two views of the launch of the 150,000 ton *Aurora* from JL Thompson's on 25th June 1975. This was the last of the big ships built on the Wear.

Above: The *Torr Head* built by Austin & Pickersgill's in 1961 for the Head Line of Bristol. It was one of five ships launched that year from the Southwick yard.

Right: One of the crew's cabins (double) on the *Torr Head*.

SD 14 – The Name Game

In the 1960s Austin & Pickersgill's designed the SD 14 to replace the ageing Liberty ships. The company's managing director, Ken Douglas, was the driving force behind the SD 14. The 14 in SD 14 referred to the 14,000 tons deadweight of the new ship but that is where agreement over the name ends. Some people say SD stands for shelter deck while others say it refers to standard design, however, a third version came from the man in charge of the project. In *Changing Tide – The Final Years of Wear Shipbuilding* Ken Douglas revealed that SD was taken from the first and last letters of Sunderland (the port's designation letters). He had originally wanted to call it Sunderland but there was already the Sunderland Flying Boat.

The 24,000 ton *Ixia* built for the Stag Line of North Shields by Austin & Pickersgill's. The bulk carrier took only 70 working days from its keel laying until its launch on 22nd July 1964.

The 26,000 ton *Cairnsmore* leaving Sunderland. She was launched from Austin & Pickersgill's on 9th October 1982.

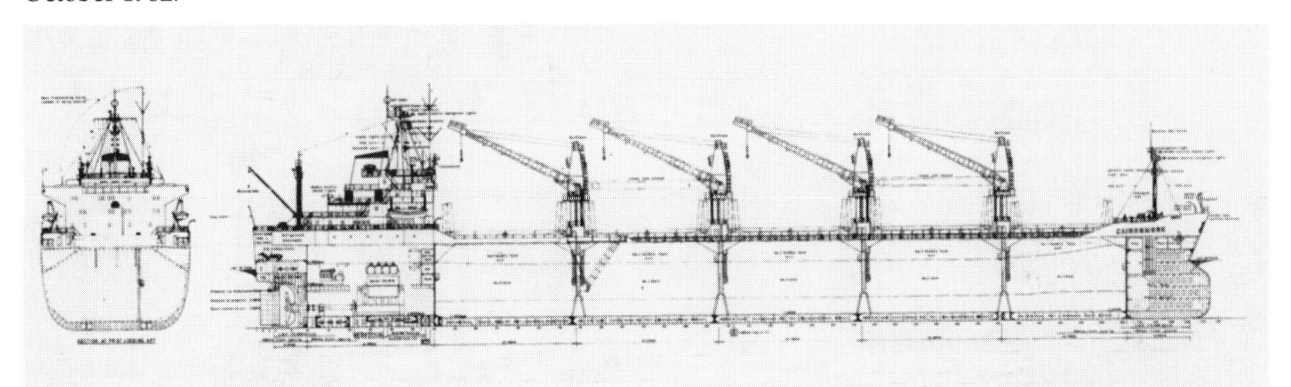

A plan of the *Cairnsmore* which was the first in a new series of bulk carriers – B35.

The crew's smoke room on board the *Cairnsmore*.

The ship's wheelhouse showing the latest technology available in the early '80s.

The Launch of the Fernriver

The 46,000 ton bulk carrier *Fernriver* ready for launch from North Sands on 16th September 1966. JL Thompson's built the ship for Fearnley and Eger of Oslo.

The launch had to be delayed for two days because of damage to one of the large cranes at the yard.

Tugs tow the *Fernriver* to the fitting-out quay.

A Good Year For Shipbuilding

The final year of the 1960s was a good one for Sunderland shipyards. Between the launch of the *Iktinos* from Doxford's on 17th January to the *Sea Moon* going down Bartram's slipway on Christmas Eve a total of 22 ships were built in the Wear yards in 1969. This was four ships more than the previous year and gross tonnage was up 46,042 from 1968 to 291,484 tons.

The three yards of the Doxford & Sunderland Group built a total of ten ships during the year. The Deptford (Laing's) yard built the tankers *Laurelwood* and *Hollywood* and the bulk carrier *Federal Lakes*. The cargo liners *Iktinos*, *Finix*, *Iason* and *Feax* were completed at the Pallion yard for Greek owners. The company's North Sands (JL Thompson's) yard launched three bulk carriers – *August Pacific*, *Amber Pacific* and *Berkshire*.

Austin & Pickersgill's and Bartram's also ended the decade on a high note. A dozen vessels were launched from the company's two yards. The South Dock (Bartrams) yard built six dry cargo vessels – *Captain Manolis*, *Sklerton*, *Prodromos*, *Virtus*, *Saint Francois* and *Sea Moon* – each of around 9,000 tons. Austin & Pickersgill's Southwick yard built the dry cargo ships *Carina*, *Ariadne*, *Janey* and *Rupert de Larrinaga* and the bulk carriers *Lawrentian* and *Helene*.

Calendar of Launches for 1969

Date	Ship	Yard
17th January	*Iktinos*	Doxford's
20th January	*Federal Lakes*	Laing's
17th February	*Captain Manolis*	Bartram's
25th February	*Carina*	Pickersgill's
7th March	*August Pacific*	Thompson's
15th April	*Sklerton*	Bartram's
16th April	*Ariadne*	Pickersgill's
18th April	*Finix*	Doxford's
29th May	*Janey*	Pickersgill's
30th May	*Prodromos*	Bartram's
31st May	*Laurelwood*	Laing's
11th July	*Rupert De Larrinaga*	Pickersgill's
16th July	*Amber Pacific*	Thompson's
27th August	*Virtus*	Bartram's
28th August	*Iason*	Doxford's
9th October	*Lawrentian*	Pickersgill's
14th October	*Hollywood*	Laing's
23rd October	*Saint Francois*	Bartram's
24th November	*Berkshire*	Thompson's
8th December	*Feax*	Doxford's
22nd December	*Helene*	Pickersgill's
24th December	*Sea Moon*	Bartram's

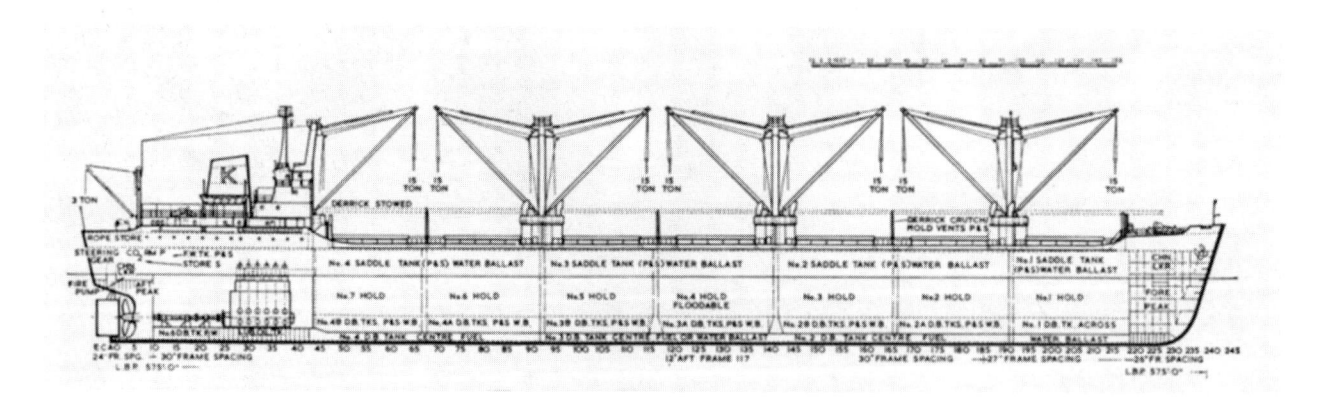

Above: The plan of the bulk carrier *Helene* with accommodation for 49 officers and crew.

Right: The *Helene* was launched from Austin & Pickersgill's on 22nd December 1969. She started her working life carrying bauxite and other minerals from Jamaica to the Gulf ports of the United States.

The 24,000 ton tanker *Laurelwood* entering the water from the Deptford yard of Doxford and Sunderland Shipbuilding and Engineering Company on Saturday 31st May 1969. The launch had been delayed for a fortnight because of a strike by 260 fitters and millwrights which in turn led to the lay off of 3,500 men at the firm's Pallion, Deptford and North Sands yards. The dispute had started with the dismissal of 22 fitters on special day shifts at North Sands. The strike was resolved with the re-instatement of the dismissed fitters. *(Courtesy of Sunderland Museum and Winter Gardens – Tyne and Wear Museums)*

Right: The *Laurelwood* at sea, the ship was charted to Mobil from owners John I. Jacobs of London.

Below: A plan of the *Laurelwood* which was designed to transport a range of petrochemical cargoes in its 19 main and four smaller tanks.

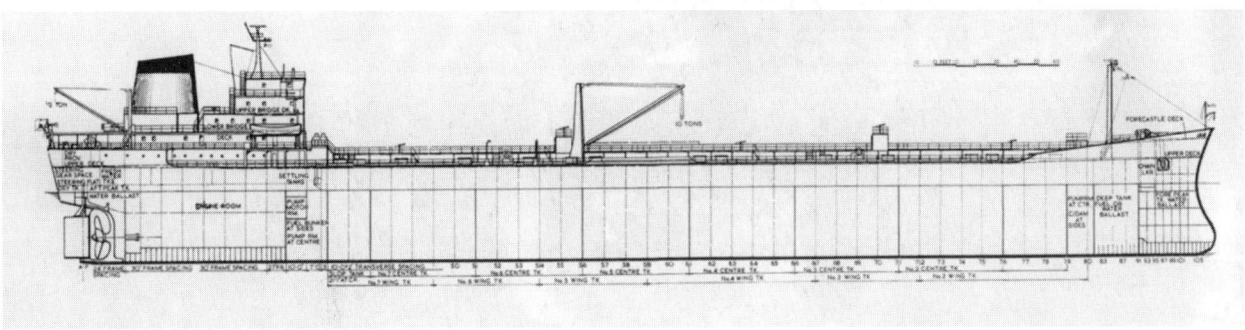

Crowds flock to the riverside to witness launches in the 1970s. The launches of these huge vessels drew large crowds to witness the spectacular event.

Chapter Four

Sport And Pastimes

Shipbuilding & Sunderland AFC

Shipbuilding played a major part in the rise of Sunderland AFC in the 1880s and '90s. It was some of the town's leading shipbuilders who were behind the club's early success. After being formed by schoolteachers in 1879 the club was soon opened up to outsiders and it was men like John Blumer and his sons William and Thomas, Robert Thompson and James Marr who took the club forward.

William Blumer helped with the club's finances when they used to play at Horatio Street in 1883-84. The ground lay not far from Blumer's shipyard and he was a regular visitor on match days. When collections were taken among spectators he always gave generously.

One of the Sunderland team that turned out at Horatio Street in the true amateur days of 1883 was half back Jack Kirtley who was chief draughtsman at Bartram's. He played in the same side as Sunderland's founding father Jimmy Allan (a teacher at Hendon Board School).

In the early years of the game payment to players was prohibited but clubs got round this by finding their players employment off the pitch. In Sunderland's case the majority of players were found work in the shipyards. Sunderland secretary John Grayston recalled how Scotsman Jimmy Hunter was the club's first covert professional. He was given a job at North Sands in February 1885 to induce him to turn out for Sunderland. Others soon followed and were given jobs at Thompson's or Blumer's yards or Dickinson's engine works. When Billy Gibson arrived from Scotland to play for Sunderland in 1888 he was not only given a job at Dickinson's but his father was also found employment at the Palmer's Hill engine works.

Robert Thompson

Scotsman G. Monaghan came south to play for Sunderland and later signed for rivals Sunderland Albion. When Albion went on tour in 1888 Monaghan was unable to travel because he had injured his back while working at Bartram's and Haswell's shipyard at the South Dock.

By the end of the 1880s those involved in committee work at the club included: Mr W. Pickersgill, head of W. Pickersgill & Son; Mr I. McLintock, time manager of Robert Thompson's at Southwick; Mr Carter, manager of John Dickinson & Sons and John Cook, a foreman joiner at Laing's yard. Even the team's trainer, Joe Bell, was a foreman at Robert Thompson's Southwick yard. Robert Thompson himself was president of Sunderland AFC and James Marr was chairman. Marr played an important role in helping Sunderland gain admittance to the Football League in 1890. The only reason Sunderland were not founder members of the Football League in 1888 was probably because of its geographical position. Marr helped persuade the original

The Sunderland team in 1885-86 season before they played in the familiar red and white stripes. At this time players were being brought in and given jobs in the town's shipyards. Jimmy Hunter, the first of these 'undercover professionals', is second from the left in the back row.

In December 1888 North Sands Shipyard Rovers played their matches on Abbs Field. Sunderland AFC had played at Abbs Field off Fulwell Road between 1884 and 1886. The Central Laundry was later built on the site and in recent years this has been replaced by new housing.

clubs (located in the Midlands and North West) to allow Sunderland to join them. This was achieved after the club said they would pay the extra travelling expenses the other clubs would incur by Sunderland joining the League.

After leaving Abbs Field in 1886 Sunderland acquired a ground at Newcastle Road. This was to be a turning point for the club that would lead on to them becoming the best team in England. When the club first took over Newcastle Road it was an undrained waterlogged field and it was with the help of men from the North Sands shipyard that terracing and stands were built there. In less than a decade at their new ground Sunderland had won three League championships.

> **Blumer's Yard**
>
> Not only did Blumer's shipyard provide employment for Sunderland players but the owner and his sons, William and Thomas, personally assisted the club. John Grayston recalled William was an ardent supporter of the team and another club secretary, William T. Wallace, recalled Thomas also took a keen interest in Sunderland.
>
> John Blumer had come to Sunderland in the 1850s from South Shields to work as a shipwright at SP Austin's. He went into business with his brother-in-law, George Booth, at North Sands. Later Blumer moved to a site nearer the sea at the North Docks to allow the expansion of William Pile's yard at North Sands.
>
> Blumer's had a reputation for turning out good quality ships and they built vessels for the Admiralty and the P&O Line.
>
> In 1895 John Blumer retired and his sons took over the running of the yard.
>
> Blumer's were hit by the shipyard slump after the First World War and two ships were left on the stocks for fours years before they could be completed. The *Usworth* was finally launched on 4th November 1926 followed by the *Cydonia* on 3rd December.

William Blumer

Thomas Blumer

Sunderland, Scotland and JL Thompson's

Ted Doig, Sunderland's Scottish international goalkeeper of the 1890s and early 1900s also found time to work as a storekeeper at JL Thompson's shipyard. The great keeper helped Sunderland to four League titles – 1891-92, 1892-93, 1894-95 and 1901-02. By the time he left to join Liverpool he had set an appearance record for Sunderland that was to last seventy years. The 1901 Census records Ted living at 17 Forster Street in Monkwearmouth with his wife and five children as well as a widowed aunt.

Ted Doig in Sunderland colours and Scotland cap.

The goalkeeper's cottage in Forster Street was just a short walk to his workplaces – JL Thompson's yard and Newcastle Road and then Roker Park.

Charity Football Matches During The First World War

Despite the importance of shipbuilding to the war effort in the First World War many men from yards on the Wear still enlisted in the Forces. Their show of patriotism was not forgotten by those who remained in the yards. On 6th November 1915 a football match between Bartram's riveters and platers was played to raise money for a Christmas Fund for the workmen who had enlisted from the yard. The match was held on the Black Watch ground at Hendon and raised £10 1s 7½d for the Fund.

On the same day shipwrights from Doxford's East Yard played the West Yard before a large crowd at the West End ground in aid of St Gabrial's V.A.D. Hospital. Another match was staged that day at St Thomas's cricket field in Hendon between Sunderland Shipbuilding Company's Munition Workers and the Northumberland Fusilliers to raise money for wounded soldiers.

In the following weeks charity matches continued to be played. These included Doxford's Caulkers East Yard v West Yard, Sunderland Shipbuilding Company's Munition Workers v Sherwood Foresters and Doxford's Quay fitters v Voluntary Munition fitters.

On 4th December 1915 Osbourne, Graham and Company officials, foremen and workmen played a charity match on Hylton Wesleyan FC ground. The money raised went on sending Christmas gifts to workmen from the firm on active service.

Ditchburn and the Bank of England Club

E.W. 'Bill' Ditchburn was one of Sunderland's most celebrated personalities in the last century. He was well known for his cabinet works in Villiers Street but he was also a partner in a boat works in the North Quay. During the 1920s Spain & Ditchburn were manufacturing life boats, dinghies, motor-boats, life-rafts, self-lubricating cargo-blocks, cooperage and ships' furnishings at their Monkwearmouth works.

Bill Ditchburn was famous as chairman of Sunderland AFC during the 'Bank of England Days' but he also encouraged his workforce to play the game (*right*).

Ditchburn was active in local politics and was Mayor of Sunderland on two occasions in the 1930s and the Ditchburn Cup was competited for by local schools into this century.

During his chairmanship of Sunderland AFC in the late 1940s and '50s money was no object as the club assembled a side to challenge the best in the land. However, these were the days of the maximum wage and the club found itself the centre of an FA investigation into illegal payments to players. Ditchburn was banned for life and although this was later overturned he never went back into football.

This team is from the mid 1930s with members of the Ditchburn family playing a prominent role in the running of their works' side. Back row, left to right: J. Aldridge (trainer), J. Ditchburn (vice-president), R. Ditchburn (vice-president), R. Weston, A. Storey (captain), R. Middleton, W. Lilley, W. Connor, J. Hulley, R. Shotton (secretary), A. Heede (chairman). Front row: R. Richardson, J. Maddison, A. Fletcher, Bill Ditchburn (president), E. Forrest and G. Crow. The team won the Sunderland J.O.C. League in 1934-35 season and retained the title the following season as well as lifting the League Cup and Horner Cup.

Raich Carter turned down the offer to join Sunderland straight from school to start an apprenticeship as an electrician at Sunderland Forge and Electrical Company. After joining the firm he played for the apprentices' team on Saturday afternoons. At seventeen he gave up his apprenticeship to sign for Sunderland. In November 1931 he swapped his nine shilling a week wage at the Forge for a £10 signing-on fee and £3 a week (£4 when he played in the Reserves). Raich Carter went on to become one of football's all-time greats and the first Sunderland skipper to lift the FA Cup.

Right: Raich Carter with his wife Rose on Cup Final day 1937.

Below: Albert Stubbins in the drawing office of Laing's shipyard during the war. Although born on Tyneside Albert was brought up in the United States. After returning to this country his career was interrupted by World War Two. During hostilities he turned out for Sunderland as a guest player and helped the club reach the wartime Cup Final in 1942. At this time he was working in the drawing office of the Sunderland yard. Albert played most of his football during the war with Newcastle United for whom he scored an incredible 245 goals in 199 appearances. After the war he was transferred to Liverpool where he became a great favourite. Albert Stubbins left a lasting impression on members of the Beatles as he is one of the personalities included on the sleeve of their Sgt Pepper album.

Sunderland AFC still had influence in getting players work in shipyards even in the 1950s. When the promising Northern Ireland winger, Billy Bingham, joined the club in 1950 he was fixed up with a job at Pickersgill's as an apprentice electrician. At this time the shipyard's company secretary, Billy Parker, was also a director of Sunderland AFC.

Billy Bingham went on to become a regular for Sunderland and Northern Ireland. He was on the losing side in two FA Cup semi-finals with Sunderland but reached Wembley after joining Luton Town. In the 1959 Final the former Pickersgill's man and his team-mates were beaten 2-1 by Nottingham Forest.

103

The TLF (Thompson's, Laing's & Forge)

As well as his work with Sunderland AFC James Marr took an interest in the welfare of the workers in his shipyards and forge. This led in 1922 to the formation of the TLF (Thompson's, Laing's and Forge) Recreation Ground and Institute in Fulwell Road.

James Marr began his working life at Oswald's Pallion yard in 1868. He moved to JL Thompson's North Sands yard where he became general manager in 1882. Five years later he established Sunderland Forge Company in partnership with other members of JL's. In 1901 he became manager director of JL's and eight years later he was invited to join the board of Laing's and went on to become chairman of the firm. He was knighted for his services to shipbuilding during the First World War.

James Marr was one of the most influential figure in Sunderland's shipbuilding and football history. In 1890 he helped Sunderland AFC gain admission to the Football League and in later years helped establish the TLF Recreation Ground and Institute.

The Fulwell Day Centre on the site of the former TLF Institute.

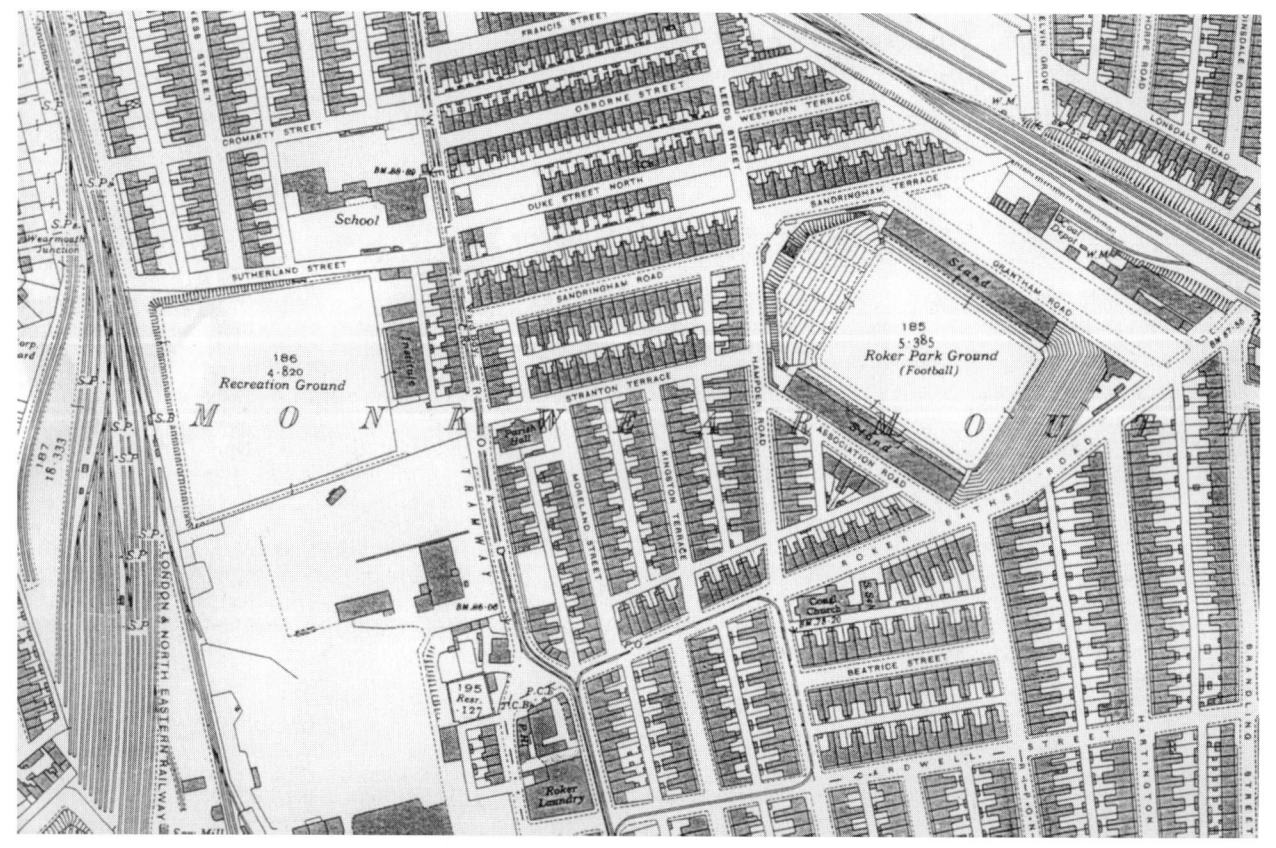

An Ordnance Survey map from 1941 showing how close the TLF Recreation Ground was to Roker Park.

Above: An Apprentice League match at the TLF between teams from Sunderland Forge and John Lynn's (in stripes) played around 1950. The John Lynn players are, left to right, Martin Monaghan, Colin Robinson and Ronnie Young.

Local author, Albert Anderson (*right*), played football at the TLF in the 1950s. He turned out for Tyzacks who played their home matches at the TLF. Albert recalled the ground was one of the best in Sunderland. For big matches, like cup finals, a sheet would be spread out at the entrance for spectators to toss coins into.

Below: A football team from Sunderland Forge in the 1950s. At this time the Forge had one of the best teams in the Apprentice League.

Shipyard Workers & The 1937 FA Cup Campaign

As Sunderland progressed in the 1937 FA Cup competition supporters dared to wonder if this was to be the year they would lift the old trophy for the first time. In the quarter-final Sunderland held Wolves at Molineux and the replay at Roker Park could still not provide a winner. A crowd of over 60,000 watched the second replay at Hillsbrough on a Monday afternoon (these were the days before floodlit matches). On the morning of the game there was heavy snow on Wearside and when men arrived in the yards at 7.30 they were told there was no work. This allowed men to travel to Sheffield for the match (some still in work clothes). Their trek was rewarded with Sunderland booking their semi-final place with a 4-0 win.

On the morning of the semi-final the shipyards should have been working but thousands of men travelled to Huddersfield for the game against Millwall. The *Sunderland Echo* reported: 'Even though the shipyards wanted their men at work there were many off – and it was not just the shortage of steel and rivets which kept them away.' The reporter found it hard to find anyone working in the yards on the day. One man he found leaving Doxford's said it would take him some time to live down the shame at home of going to work instead of the match!

Victory over Millwall set up Sunderland's first visit to Wembley Stadium and shipyard workers were out in force again in the capital. Those lucky enough to get tickets saw Sunderland win the Cup for the first time in their long history with a 3-1 victory over Preston North End.

Rowers on the river with Laing's Deptford yard in the background. This was no ordinary rowing crew – they were coal trimmers using shovels as oars.

Sunderland has always been proud of its football – and not only matches played at Roker Park or the Stadium of Light. The game was just as popular in the shipyards with many great teams made up of workers. As well as senior sides, Sunderland had a strong apprentice league made up of shipyard and engineering firms. However, playing was not restricted to Saturdays and organized competitions. There were many games, just as competitive, played during a dinner hour.

Right and below: 'On me head son' – men of all ages enjoy a game of football at JL Thompson's in the 1960s. The deck of the *Borgsten* provided one of the more unusual playing surfaces for this dinner hour game.

From Austin & Pickersgill's To Wembley Stadium

Austin & Pickersgill's Engineering Buyer in the 1970s, Gerry Donoghue, was one of the best non-League footballers in the North East. Despite playing for Sunderland Boys, Gerry signed for Newcastle United in 1962. After one season he decided to opt out of his contract with United and play part-time football. He joined South Shields and stayed with the Mariners for nine years. In 1972 Gerry joined Scarborough and within a year had helped them win the FA Trophy (this had replaced the FA Amateur Cup) at Wembley Stadium. He played for Blyth Spartans for a year before returning to Scarborough to achieve more success in the FA Trophy. Part of his fitness programme at this time included training sessions at Austin & Pickersgill's during his dinner hour. Gerry later helped coach Sunderland Youth team.

Left: Gerry at work at Austin & Pickersgill's.

Gerry Donoghue (centre) in the early '60s when he played for Fulwell CAYS.

Pigeon Fanciers

Pigeon racing was at one time a popular pastime with shipyard workers. One of the most successful pigeon fanciers was John Richardson, a shipwright at Austin & Pickersgill's, who started his loft in 1964. *The Racing Pigeon* magazine reported: 'John Richardson of Plains Farm is a fancier in the top class of the Up North Combine, with an extraordinary talent for winning against all opposition at all levels of competition. His family of birds are mainly medium to large. They are excellent handlers and are in tip-top condition, better-conditioned at this time of year than most fanciers have them at any time during the racing season. Flying in the big Sunderland Federation, John's positions are numerous and in the Up North Combine his share of wins is well above most people's dreams.'

Many lofts overlooked the shipyards such as those at Southwick that faced Laing's yard on the opposite bank of the river.

Survivalists

In 1982 four workers from Austin & Pickersgill's took part in a nine day 'sponsored survival' in Middleton-in-Teesdale. The money raised by Keith Reay, John McLaughlin, Shaun Carolan and Barry Douthwaite was divided between a charity for mentally handicapped children in Sunderland and the RNLI. They did not have tents and had to live on what they gathered or caught. Berries, fish and rabbits were some of the food on the menu for the intrepid A&P men in the wilds of Teesdale.

Shipwright John McLaughlin enjoying the outdoor life on a break from Austin & Pickersgill's.

Chapter Five

Tales Of The Riverbank

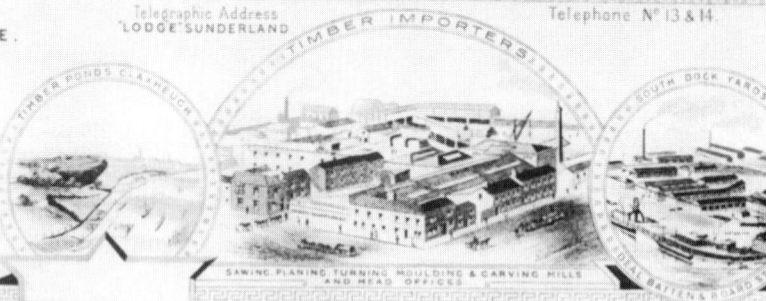

An advertisement for Joseph Thompson's timber yard in 1929.

Three advertisements from the 1850s for firms supplying local shipyards.

Two-Thirds of a Ship

The launch of the *Armilla* from JL Thompson's on 7th March 1947 produced one of the Wear's more unusual sights as the *Armilla* was only two-thirds of a ship. The original *Armilla* had been built 16 years before on the Tyne but corrosion to the hull and tanks caused by carrying benzine left only the stern of the vessel worth salvaging. The novel solution was to build a new fore part and centre and join it to the old stern to form a new oil tanker. The joining of the old and new was completed at Greenwell's dry dock within a few months and floated out (*below*). When the new *Armilla* was handed over to the Anglo-Saxon Petroleum Company she was 4,000 tons larger and 30 feet longer than the original vessel.

Two views of work on the conversion of the oil vessel *Balder* at Manor Quay.

George Clark's

Above: George Clark's Engine Works before the First World War. George Clark started his engineering business in the mid nineteenth century and in 1854 built the first marine engine in Sunderland – fitted into the *Alfred* built by Laing's. In 1872 George Clark's moved to a site in Southwick where they were to stay for almost 100 years. The works became a familiar site on the Wear with its towering hammer-head crane capable of lifting 100 tons.

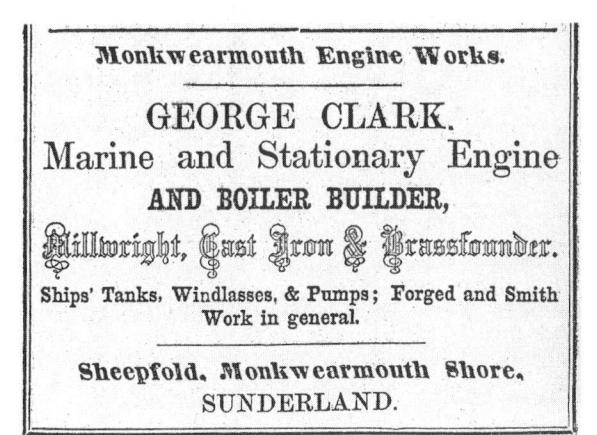

Monkwearmouth Engine Works.

GEORGE CLARK,
Marine and Stationary Engine
AND BOILER BUILDER,
Millwright, Cast Iron & Brassfounder.

Ships' Tanks, Windlasses, & Pumps; Forged and Smith Work in general.

Sheepfold, Monkwearmouth Shore,
SUNDERLAND.

Above: An early advert for George Clark's from 1859.

Right: An advert for the engine works from 1907. Sixty years later this well-known Sunderland company closed its doors for the last time. Its landmark crane spent its final days under the banner of Austin's & Pickersgill's.

Above: The Robson & Croudace timber mills in the South Dock. The first half of the nineteenth century was the heyday for timber yards like these. They supplied the shipyards that crammed the riverside at this time and turned out wooden sailing ships of all sizes. Even the advent of iron and steel ships in the second half of the century did not end the important role timber yards played in the shipbuilding industry. *Below*: An advert for Robson's timber yard in 1929.

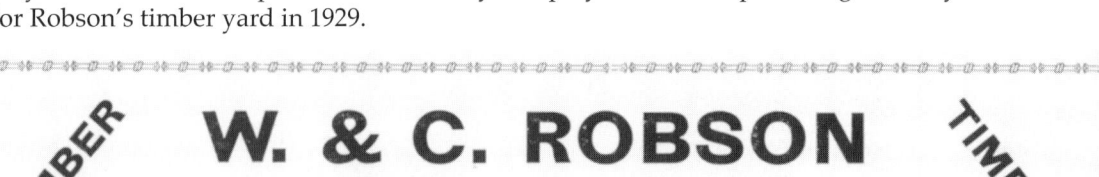

TIMBER

W. & C. ROBSON

TIMBER

TIMBER IMPORTERS

SAWING, PLANING AND MOULDING MILLS

Telegrams
"Roson, Sunderland."

SOUTH DOCKS, SUNDERLAND

Telephone: 491

Established Over 70 Years

Every Description of Timber supplied to Shipbuilders, Engineers, Contractors, Collieries, etc.

Wire Rope Manufacturers

There were a number of firms in Sunderland which supplied the shipbuilding industry.

Hendon-based Glaholm & Robson was one of the largest wire rope manufacturers in the country between the wars. An advert from the 1930s noted its output included steel wire ropes of the following types: galvanized flexible and extra flexible ropes for ships' hawsers, towlines, rigging and deck gear, launching, slipways, salvage and dredging.

Another rope manufacturer was Webster's who had an ideal riverside location situated between Laing's and Doxford's. As well as local yards, Webster's were also contractors to the Admiralty.

Right: An advert for Glaholm & Robson from the 1930s.

This unusual view shows how much wire rope was needed for the Doxford-built *Pikebank* in the 1970s.

Above: A view of the erecting shop at J. Dickinson & Sons' Engine Works at Palmer's Hill between the wars. This firm was founded in the 1850s and made marine engines and ship boilers. After the Second World War the works were taken over by Doxford's.

Right: An advert for the North Eastern Marine Engineering Company from 1928. At this time the firm had already been in business for over sixty years.

SUPREMACY

ESTABLISHED over 60 years ago, we still claim to hold a supremacy as Builders of All Types of Ship-Propelling Machinery of First-Class Manufacture.

Our message to you is one of confidence in our ability to supply reliable, economic, and efficient machinery at a genuinely low market rate.

We solicit your inquiries for any of the following:—

"North-Eastern" Diesel Engines, Triple or Quadruple Expansion Steam Engines, Turbines, and Marine Boilers. "North-Eastern" Smoke Tube Super-Heaters for new machinery or for installation in existing vessels, Evaporators, Feed Water Heaters and Cleaners, Donkey Pumps, Internal Steam Separators for Boilers, etc., and Machinery Repairs of any Description. Specialists in "Perlit" Iron Castings for High Temperature and Pressure Engines.

THE NORTH EASTERN MARINE ENGINEERING COMPANY LIMITED
SUNDERLAND.

Sunderland Marine Engine Builders and Repairers

The *Port of Sunderland Guide* for 1948 listed the marine engine builders and repairers in Sunderland at that time:

Name of Firm	Location	Length of Quay Feet	Number of Fitting-out Berths
George Clark (1938) Limited	Southwick	700	1
William Doxford & Sons Ltd	Pallion	600	2
	Palmer's Hill Quay	600	2
The North Eastern Marine Engineering Company (1938) Limited	South Docks	500	2

Above: Painters ready for work at JL Thompson's yard.

Right: An advert for Camrex paints from the 1930s. This Sunderland firm provided paint for local shipyards.

Members of a shipping squad at Laing's in the late 1970s. Alexander Marrs is on the right and his brother George is second from the left. The shipping squad travelled around all the different yards supplying them with materials like paint and welding rods.

Greenwell's Dry Dock

Above: An aerial view of Greenwell's in the 1960s with two ships in dry dock.

Greenwell's was founded by T.W. Greenwell in 1901 and became the most successful ship repairers on the Wear. In the 1920s the firm built a dry dock which was 500 feet long and 75 feet wide. At the same time they had a 600 feet repair quay constructed.

Above: Preparations being made to receive a vessel in one of Greenwell's dry docks.

Greenwell's became specialists in tanker repairs. In later years they used three dry docks that were of lengths of 675 feet, 565 feet and 357 feet. The deep water quay was extended to 800 feet in length.

Left: Inside the platers' shop at Greenwell's repair works in the 1960s.

Greenwell's dry dock between the wars.

An advert for Greenwell's from after the Second World War.

Above: The *Maid of Orleans* in Boulogne in 1959 ready to depart for Folkestone. This photograph was taken by the well known Sunderland photographer and author Ian S. Carr. Eleven years later the cross channel ferry came to Greenwell's dry dock for an overhaul and Ian was there to capture the *Maid of Orleans* again. This time he was able to show a full view of the vessel (*right*).

Mergers and Nationalisation

After the Second World War a number of companies on the Wear joined forces to form the Sunderland Shipbuilding Dry Docks & Engineering Company Ltd. The combined company, including the shipyards of JL Thompson's and Laing's, later became known as the Sunderland Shipbuilding Group.

In 1961 Doxford's amalgamated with this group and the company became the Doxford & Sunderland Shipbuilding & Engineering Group. Ten years later the group was taken over by Court Line and renamed Sunderland Shipbuilders Ltd. However, the collapse of Court Line led to Doxford's, Thompson's and Laing's coming under Government control. In 1977 the shipbuilding industry was nationalised and Austin & Pickersgill's joined the three other yards to become part of British Shipbuilders.

The entrance to JL Thompson's in the late 1970s. At this time the yard was under the banner of Sunderland Shipbuilders.

North East Shipbuilders Ltd
A subsidiary of British Shipbuilders

PO Box 9
Sunderland
SR4 6UQ

Telephone: 091 510 0055
Telex: 53165
Fax: 091 565 0442

In the final days of shipbuilding on the Wear the Sunderland yards became part of North East Shipbuilders Ltd. This group included Smith's Dock on the Tees.

Sunderland Shipbuilding Group

An advert from around 1960 listed the firms in the Sunderland Shipbuilding Group and their operations:

JL Thompson & Sons Ltd
Shipbuilders and ship repairers

Sir James Laing & Sons Ltd
Shipbuilders and brass founders

The Sunderland Forge & Engineering Company Ltd
Electric winches, motors, generators, switchboards, complete electrical installations, propeller shafts and other forgings

TW Greenwell & Company Ltd
Ship repairers

John Lynn & Company Ltd
Steam winches, hydraulic winches and capstans

Wolsingham Steel Company Ltd
Steel frames, rudders and general steel castings

Sunderland Engineering Equipment Company Ltd
Light engineering

Wear Winch & Foundry Company Ltd
Hand reels and winches, iron castings up to 10 tons

An advert for the Pallion works of John Lynn, from around 1950, which was part of the Sunderland Shipbuilding Group.

The SuperShuttle Ferry

The *Superflex November* is floated out of Doxford's yard in November 1988. The ship was the last to be built on the Wear.

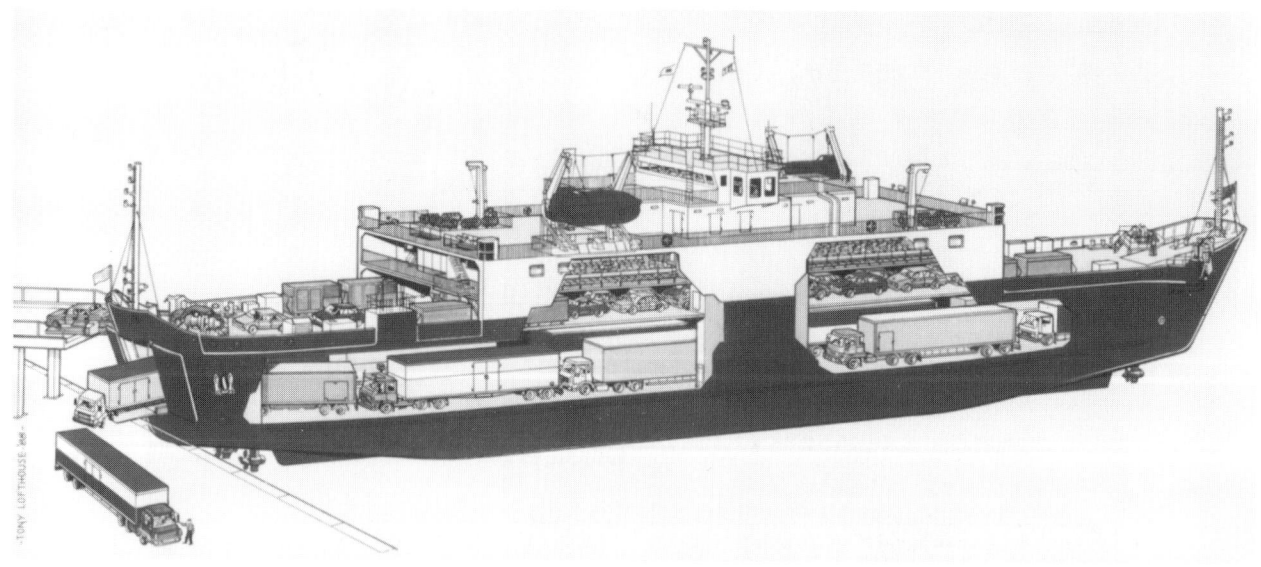

An artist's impression of the ferry full to capacity. An information pack produced by British Shipbuilders as a guide to potential buyers stated:

'SuperShuttle Ferry – An innovative concept in the design of economical, flexible and reliable ferries for vehicle and passenger shuttle traffic. SuperShuttle is built by North East Shipbuilders Ltd based in Sunderland on the River Wear. As a class it raises new standards for ferry design and construction; it has already been successfully tried and tested in operation. Designed to carry all kinds of ro-ro cargoes together with passengers, SuperShuttle is constructed for inter-island and coastal trade …

The principle qualities of SuperShuttle are: Outstanding manoeuvrability – low manning – reliability – ease of maintenance – flexible, high payload – minimal fuel consumption – vehicle loading/unloading without turning – no dry docking necessary for equipment/machinery repairs and maintenance – shallow draught operation.'

The sea trials of one of the last ships to be built on the Wear – a car ferry built in the late 1980s.

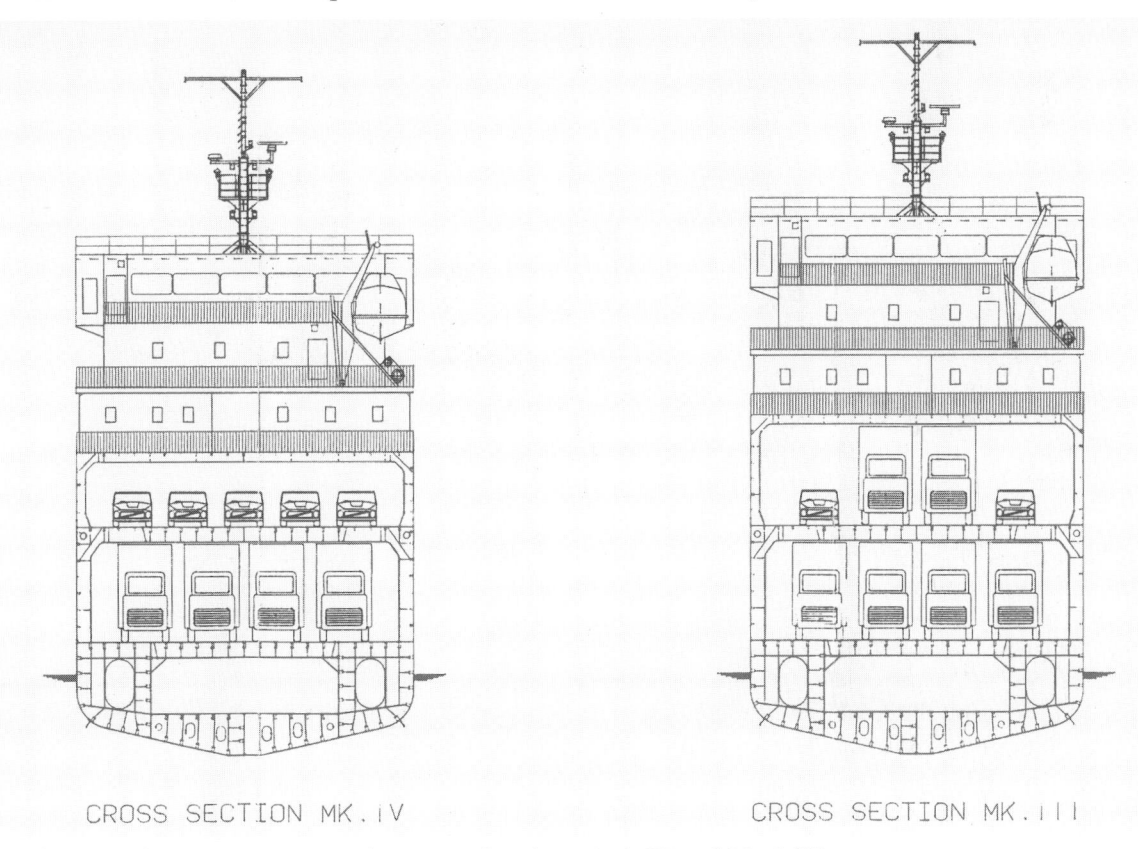

CROSS SECTION MK.IV   CROSS SECTION MK.III

A plan showing the two versions of the SuperShuttle – Mark III and Mark IV.

This photograph shows how diverse shipbuilding had become in its final years in Sunderland. Three different types of ship are tied up on the Wear while in the distance a 'rig' can be seen in the North Dock.

Two views of the *Interocean II* in the North Dock. This towering structure became for a time a new landmark on Sunderland's skyline.

Above: Looking up river during the final years of shipbuilding in Sunderland.

Right: The *Stena Wellserver* alongside a car ferry in the 1980s. The unwanted ferries were berthed on the Wear for months.

The dismantling of the former crane of George Clark's.

Left: The demolition of Austin & Pickersgill's in 1991. Across the river the covered building halls of Doxford's escaped this fate but have not returned to shipbuilding.

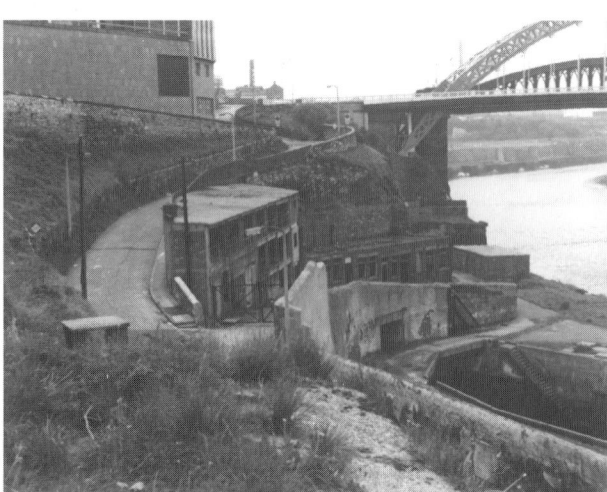

Two views of the old Austin's shipyard and repair yard in a state of dereliction. The photograph on the right shows the cranes of JL Thompson's across the river.

Left: The giant crane at JL Thompson's meets its end and the crane at Manor Quay (*above*) would soon follow.

Below: The old JL Thompson's yard being cleared. The University of Sunderland's St Peter's Campus and the National Glass Centre now occupy the site.

Two Sunderland Shipbuilders' ships on trials off the Northumberland coast. The 70,000 ton bulk carrier *Orient City*, in the foreground, was launched from Laing's on 24th November 1976. The 16,925 ton cargo liner *Streambank* was floated out of Doxford's covered yard at Pallion on 18th February 1977. The ships are on the 'Newbiggin Mile' where their average speed was calculated over two runs.